Women
and Worship

Women and Worship

*A Guide to Non-Sexist Hymns,
Prayers, and Liturgies*

SHARON NEUFER EMSWILER
AND
THOMAS NEUFER EMSWILER

HARPER & ROW, PUBLISHERS
New York, Hagerstown, San Francisco, London

WOMEN AND WORSHIP: A Guide to Non-Sexist Hymns, Prayers, and Liturgies. Copyright © 1974 by Sharon Neufer Emswiler and Thomas Neufer Emswiler. All rights reserved. Printed in the United States of America. No part of this book may be used or reproduced in any manner whatsoever without written permission except in the case of brief quotations embodied in critical articles and reviews. For information address Harper & Row, Publishers, Inc., 10 East 53rd Street, New York, N.Y. 10022. Published simultaneously in Canada by Fitzhenry & Whiteside Limited, Toronto.

Designed by Gwendolyn O. England

Library of Congress Cataloging in Publication Data

Emswiler, Sharon Neufer.
  Women and Worship.

  Bibliography: p.
  1. Liturgies. 2. Public worship. 3. Women in Christianity. I. Emswiler, Thomas Neufer, joint author. II. Title.
BV198.E57   264   73–18681
ISBN 0–06–062245–8
ISBN 0–06–062246–6 (pbk.)

78 79 80 81 82 10 9 8 7 6 5 4 3

*To all those who are struggling to make
the liberating presence of Christ more real
in our churches*

Contents

Introduction

THIS BOOK grew out of pain and hope. The pain belongs to women who have begun to discover that for centuries they have been forced to receive their identity from men rather than from God. The hope is that women are beginning to break free from their bondage to subservient roles as they discover the profound potential within them. For those of us who call ourselves Christians, this new freedom must find expression in our worship. If it does not, our worship will no longer be an honest presentation of what we believe about life, and increasing numbers of women and men will find themselves alienated from all that the traditional Church stands for.

This book was written to try to provide guidelines for those who wish to learn how to develop creative, meaningful non-sexist worship. It is intended not just for the concerned minister or professional worship leader but also for lay women and men who want to participate actively in changing attitudes of worship in their churches.

In order to deal most responsibly with this subject, we have made several assumptions about you, the reader. We assume that you are at least mildly concerned about the importance of language in worship. We also assume that you hope that the language of worship can be redesigned in such a way as to bring maximum meaning to as many people as possible. Further, we assume that you have noticed or had called to your attention that most worship language used in worship services is sexist, that is, it is heavily overloaded with masculine references—"brother," "sons of God," "mankind," and so forth. Finally, we are assuming that you want to do something about this sexism.

If, however, you are not sure whether you should bother to try to go ahead and do something about sexist worship, read

1

Chapter 1. You'll discover how painfully offensive most worship is today to women who are struggling to discover their unique humanness in a male-dominated world.

If you recognize the reality of sexism within most worship but are "hung up" on the theological and historical arguments regarding the validity of substituting new language, you should read Chapters 2 and 3. Chapter 2 will help you to discover that the basic biblical witness offers a clear mandate to those of us who wish to develop a new way of talking about the faith. Chapter 3 will help you to see that a "god" encased in male-dominated language is too small to be GOD and that our understanding of God can be expanded as we are able to see beyond male and female images.

The "how to" portions of this book begin with Chapter 4. Here and in the following chapters we attempt to share with you examples of our own attempts to liberate liturgy.

Also it is important for you to recognize that in this book we are not attempting to present a complete theology of worship. Many other books, such as *New Forms of Worship* by James F. White and *The Future Present* by Marianne H. Micks, already do this job admirably. Our emphasis here is on giving you practical concepts and examples so that you will be able to take a form of worship you can already justify theologically and change it so it is no longer sexist.

This book is, of course, only a beginning. It represents where we are on our own journey toward new consciousness and creative liturgy. Our hope is that you can take some of our ideas and use them to begin to "redeem" your local situation with your own creative, non-sexist liturgy.

❖1❖

How the New Woman Feels in the Old Worship Service

by Sharon Neufer Emswiler

WORSHIP IS at the very heart of the Christian life. It is the pulsating center from which we receive God's love and strength for all that we are and do. Like the blood that flows through our bodies, we keep returning to that heart for refreshment and renewal. But what happens when the heart fails to function correctly? For an increasing number of women the heart of our lives as Christians is no longer providing the meaning and power we so desperately need. Why is this so? Perhaps the best way to answer this question would be for me to describe my feelings as a woman participating in an average worship service.

I enter the sanctuary and am directed to my seat by an usher, always male, except on "Ladies' Day," that one day in the year when women are given the opportunity to "play usher." As I sit and meditate I listen to the organ prelude. If the church is a small one, I notice that the organist is a woman. However, if the church is a large, prestigious one, with an expensive organ, the position of organist is most often filled by a man.

The minister (or ministers)—male, of course—then appears to begin the service, accompanied by a lay person (male) acting as the liturgist of the morning. The call to worship is given, setting the worship service in motion. One such call to worship that

3

sticks in my mind from a service I attended contains the line, "To be is to be a brother." Hearing those words, I instantly carry them to their logical conclusion: "I am not, and never will be, a brother. Therefore, I am not. I do not exist." The service is off to a great start!

The congregation now rises for the first hymn and I find myself singing a song such as "Men and Children Everywhere" (I wonder in which group I am to include myself), "Rise Up, O Men of God," or "Faith of Our Fathers." If it is near Christmas, the selections might be "God Rest Ye, Merry Gentlemen" or "Good Christian Men, Rejoice"; while the Easter season offers such choices as "Sing With All the Sons of Glory" or "Good Christian Men Rejoice and Sing." Other possible hymns in the service might include "Once to Every Man and Nation," "Now Praise We Great and Famous Men," "Brother Man, Fold to Thy Heart," "As Men of Old Their First Fruits Bought," or "Turn Back, O Man."

If the service is of a more contemporary style, I go in the hope that the hymns will speak to me in a way that the traditional ones do not. But here, too, I discover that while the folk tunes have a great appeal to me, I am asked to sing songs with titles like "Be a New Man," "Sons of God," "Come, My Brothers," "Brothers, Get Yourselves Together," and "Brother, How's Your Love."

As I sing I try to imagine that these songs are speaking to me, but I am not accustomed to thinking of myself as a "man" or a "brother"; and the identification is difficult, and most often impossible. The only way I can find to identify with these masculine words is to attempt either to deny or set aside my femininity. But I do not want to deny that part of my personhood; I want rather to affirm it. I want my femaleness recognized and affirmed by the Church also. As the worship progresses through the prayers, creeds, and sermon, the same language form keeps recurring—always the masculine when referring to people; always the masculine when referring to God. While I sing and during prayer I change the word "men" to "people"; "mankind" to "humankind"; "sons" to "children"; "Father" to "Parent," but I feel as though I am outshouted by the rest of the congregation. My words are swallowed up by theirs.

Listening to the minister preach his sermon for the morning, I am aware that he is not really attempting to address me or my sisters in the congregation. His illustrations all revolve around men and speak overwhelmingly to the masculine experience in our society. Suddenly, I feel as though I am eavesdropping on a conversation labled "For Men Only." Or worse yet, I feel that the suspicion I had after the call to worship is true. I do not exist! I look down at my hands and arms and feet. I can see them; they are very real to me. But I feel that somehow I must be invisible to this preacher who has designed this service and now stands in front of me, speaking of "the brethren" and telling his congregation to be "new men."

Following the sermon, the worshippers are invited to participate in the celebration of the Lord's Supper. As the large group of male ushers marches down the aisle to receive the communion elements and distribute them to the congregation, I am suddenly struck with the irony of the situation. The chicken suppers, the ham suppers, the turkey suppers in the church are all prepared and served by the women. But not the Lord's Supper! Yes, it is prepared by the women, but the privilege of serving the Lord's Supper in worship is reserved for the men. This particular morning I find it very difficult to swallow the bread and drink the wine, knowing that within the Body of Christ, the Church, the sisters of Christ are not given the same respect and privileges as are his brothers.

By this point in the service I am feeling extremely uneasy, almost as though I am suffocating. I want very much for the hour to come to an end so that I can run to the door and breathe

the fresh air. Then I will know once again that I do exist, that I am alive, that I am not invisible.

When the worship hour is concluded I leave the church wondering, "Why am I going away feeling less human than when I came?" That which should have created a sense of wholeness in me made me feel dehumanized, less than a full person. What was meant to be a time of worship of the true God was, for me, a worship of the masculine—the masculine experience among humans and the masculine dimension of God.

In yet other ways male leadership in the worship of most of the larger mainline denominations reflects what society believes to be masculine. The worship in these churches is reasoned, intellectual, and often cold, lacking the emotional warmth and spontaneity more common to the feminine experience. When the presence and participation of women is reflected in the liturgy or in the sermon, it is done so in a patronizing and condescending manner, assuming stereotyped roles for us in the family, Church, and society. Women are not recognized as mature adults with abilities and interests as great and varied as those of men.

I know that I am not alone in my reactions to most Christian worship services. On occasions when I have been leading the liturgy in a worship service and have included the appropriate feminine word along with the masculine one that is written in the liturgy, women have often expressed their appreciation. They are pleased that someone has recognized their presence.

For me, the most momentous occasion showing women's feeling toward the total use of masculine terminology in worship was a service in which all of the participants were women and all the words for humans and for God were feminine. At first we felt rather silly and somewhat rebellious substituting "sisterhood" for "brotherhood" and "she" for "he" when speaking of God. But as we moved through the service the mood began to change to seriousness and excitement, reaching a climax at the conclusion of the Scripture reading in which it was said that God's covenant was given to "Sarah and her daughters." The women received those words with spontaneous applause and joyous laughter. Never before had I heard that kind of response to a Scripture reading! It was as though we women were hearing those words for the very first time in our lives. God's promise extended to *us*, the daughters of the faith.

If you are a man reading this and still are not convinced of the need for more inclusive terms in our liturgical language, or if you are a woman who has not experienced any difficulty with the predominance of masculine words, try this experiment: Turn to I John 2:9–11 and read it aloud. Now read it aloud again substituting the appropriate feminine word every time a masculine word is given. Do you *feel* any difference in your reaction to that passage when using feminine terminology? Do you, as a man, feel as close to the meaning of that passage when reading it the second time? Do you, as a woman, feel closer or further from it when using the feminine words? Try the same experiment with other books, particularly ones that use the generic "man" in abundance as do most theology books.

The words we use in worship are important also because of the *images* they form in our minds. When we hear the word "man" or "brother" or "son," the image in our mind is most often a masculine image rather than a feminine one. Because these same words are used in reference to the male specific as well as the generic, the masculine becomes much more closely associated with it in our minds. Therefore, the tendency is to form a masculine image when hearing a statement such as "If any *man* is in Christ, *he* is a new creature." The image most of us form is likely to be of a male "man" rather than a female "man." Because the masculine is the image we carry in relation to that word "man," we subconsciously receive a different message than the one actually intended, a message much more closely tied to the male than to the female human being. When a male or female is constantly bombarded with masculine terminology and masculine imagery, the result is to form the conclusion, unconsciously, that all life is lived in the masculine gender, by the male sex, thus placing the female outside the boundaries of *human* life, in a world of her own. This conclusion is strengthened by the fact that the words for the male specific, "man," and the words "human" or "human being" are interchangeable; thus woman stands apart from human.

Another problem raised by using "man" and "men" to denote both males and females is that the woman is not sure when she is supposed to be included and when she is not. Sometimes the context of the statement is a clue. "We need some men to help move the pulpit and lectern following the service this morning," most likely means "males." "All mankind is one brotherhood" probably is intended to include women as well. However, statements like "All men are created equal" and "God calls men to the ministry" leave some question in our minds. "All men are created equal" is *said* to include women but in practice is often interpreted to mean "all males." "God calls men to the ministry" leaves a woman wondering whether women are not called or whether at this particular moment she is to consider herself and all women as "men." The perceptive woman soon discovers that while she has been told that "man" generically used includes her, in practice it is often interpreted to mean "Males Only." The ambiguity of the terms allows women to think they are included while in reality they often are definitely excluded.

Language has a powerful influence on our lives; it is not a trivial matter. Words form the bridges from one human being to another. We must always strive to see that these bridges go where we want them to go and that they are kept in good repair. When words no longer communicate what we thought they did or what we want them to communicate, it is time to use other words or even create new ones to express ourselves. This is what the Church is being called to do in the language of its worship.

✤2✤

The Biblical Witness—
Stumbling Block
or Steppingstone?

THE BIBLE HAS often been used to support the status quo and in no area is this more true than in the role and rights of women. This practice runs contrary, however, to the basic message of Jesus, which calls for change—change in the lives of human beings and thus change in the world as a whole. To seek to keep things as they are because that's the way they've always been is contrary to the gospel message. God is always working for positive change. If we would work with God, we too must seek to transform the world and do away with those attitudes, customs, and theologies which are demeaning and dehumanizing to God's children, female or male.

One of the most common ways in which the Bible has been used against women, and thus misused, is by singling out specific passages which seem to portray women as inferior and holding up this idea as the absolute word of God. This amounts to a veritable worship of the biblical passage rather than of God, herself/himself—a kind of bibliolatry. God's revelation to human beings, including the biblical writers, is always distorted by our humanness, our imperfection, our own sinfulness. To say that every single passage in the Bible is the absolute truth of God is to claim unerring perception of God on the part of human beings, as well as to deify the cultural circumstances in which the revelation was given.

9

The Bible can be viewed somewhat like the proverbial forest that one can't see for the trees. By treating each and every passage as having equal value and significance to every other one, without ever looking at the main thrusts, the basic themes, one misses the larger meaning of what is said throughout the Bible.

In addition to using the Bible to justify the status quo, people have also used it to put women down. Beginning with the book of Genesis and the creation story, both men and women alike have interpreted the role and status of women to be inferior to that of men. Woman was created last (according to Genesis 2) and therefore she is of lesser importance in the eyes of God, being something of an afterthought. (Undoubtedly if Adam had been created last, he would still have been seen as having greater importance, being considered the very pinnacle of creation. In fact, the argument is often used that the human is greater than the other animals because Adam was created last, after all the rest of creation. If we follow that line of reasoning, should we not carry it out to its logical conclusion and say that woman is superior to man because she was created last?)

If the creation story is understood by Christians to be the theological basis for woman's inferiority to man, what then is to be done with the account of creation given in Genesis 1:26–31? For here woman is not created last but at the same time as man. If the fact of Eve's creation at a later point in time than Adam's and her being created out of Adam (Genesis 2:21–23) is proof positive of woman's inferiority, ought not her creation at the same time and from the same source as Adam (Genesis 1:26–31) be proof of her equality with men?

It is not surprising that the male-dominated early Christian Church sought to ignore the account in Genesis 1 when referring to the creation story as the theological basis for woman's inferiority. "Let a woman learn in silence with all submissiveness. I permit no woman to teach or to have authority over men; she is to keep silent. *For Adam was formed first, then Eve* [our italics]; and Adam was not deceived, but the woman was deceived and became a transgressor" (I Timothy 2:11-14). Here Eve's later appearance on earth is tied to the "fall," for which she is given the total blame.

In Paul's first letter to the Corinthians, the second creation story is cited as justification for woman's lesser status. "For a man ought not to cover his head, since he is the image and glory of God; but woman is the glory of man. (For man was not made from woman, but woman from man. Neither was man created for woman, but woman for man)" I Corinthians 11:7-9. In all of this, the creation story from Genesis 1 is totally ignored. However it is not in Genesis 2, but only in Genesis 1 where the male and female are created together, that man (humanity) is affirmed to be made in God's image.

It is significant, then, that when Jesus refers to the creation story (in relation to marriage), he refers to the Genesis 1 account, saying, "But *from the beginning* [our italics] of creation, 'God made them male and female' " (Mark 10:6). Clearly he understood male and female to have been created equal "from the beginning."

Paul does go on, however, to attempt to counteract what he has just said. "Nevertheless, in the Lord woman is not independent of man nor man of woman: for as woman was made from man, so man is now born of woman. And all things are from God" (I Corinthians 11:11-12).

Why is it that still today in our churches when the creation story is talked about and taught to little children it is almost always the second of the two stories that is told? Many people, including adults, are not even aware that another version of the story appears in the Bible. One can clearly see that the way we use the Bible greatly influences what we hear the Bible saying. If we totally ignore one of the creation stories, rather than holding them both in tension, we are likely to get a distorted message.

The passages which have caused the most controversy and

the most oppression for women are the ones which are usually attributed to the apostle Paul. Some of these passages undoubtedly were not written by Paul but by others, perhaps disciples of Paul. No matter who wrote them, however, they still have a great deal of power and authority for a large number of people in our churches today. Let's take a look at some of them.

The passage that is quoted frequently by those who would support the superiority of the male is one to which we have already referred, I Timothy 2:11–15: "Let a woman learn in silence with all submissiveness. I permit no woman to teach or to have authority over men; she is to keep silent. For Adam was formed first, then Eve; and Adam was not deceived, but the woman was deceived and became a transgressor. Yet woman will be saved through bearing children, if she continues in faith and love and holiness, with modesty." We not only have the subordination of women held up as part of God's divine plan, stemming from only one of the creation accounts, but we have here a new addition to the gospel: Woman shall be saved through bearing children—if she also continues in the faith. This theology seems to be quite far removed from that of Jesus, who never once made mention of such a prerequisite for the salvation of women. In fact, when such an understanding was merely hinted at, Jesus quickly corrected it. To the woman in the crowd who shouted, "Blessed is the womb that bore you, and the breasts that you sucked!" Jesus responded, "Blessed rather are those who hear the word of God and keep it!" (Luke 11:27b–28). Jesus saw no division in the requirements for men and women. Both were to be judged according to the same standards.

Another troublesome passage is found in Ephesians. Here the writer says, "Be subject to one another out of reverence for Christ. Wives, be subject to your husbands, as to the Lord. For the husband is the head of the wife as Christ is the head of the church, his body, and is himself its Savior. As the church is subject to Christ, so let wives also be subject in everything to their husbands. Husbands, love your wives, as Christ loved the church and gave himself up for her . . ." (Ephesians 5:21–26). Most people who use this verse as a model for the Christian marriage forget to read verse 21 which says that the general principal being outlined is that of *mutual* subjection. "Be subject *to one another* [our italics] out of reverence for Christ." They also ignore the meaning of the special injunction to husbands to love their wives "as Christ loved the church and gave himself up for her." The wife subjects herself to her husband because he first subjected himself to her ("We love because he first loved us"). Is not the author entreating the husband to be subject to the wife as much as the wife to the husband? In addition to interpreting the entire passage as one which is calling for the total domination of husbands over wives, a common error has been to carry the generalization beyond the marriage roles and insist upon the total submission of *all* women to *all* men. Surely that is not the intent of this passage.

A third and similar passage is found in the third chapter of Colossians in which the writer exhorts, "Wives, be subject to your husbands, as is fitting in the Lord. Husbands, love your wives, and do not be harsh with them" (Colossians 3:18–19). Here again, the specific situation is the marital one and cannot be applied to the relationship of women and men beyond marriage. What is true for the husband-wife relationship need not be true for all relationships between the sexes. But, further, what we are reading about here is the accepted husband-wife relationship of an extremely partiarchal society which existed 2,000 years ago, not necessarily the God-ordained order of male-female husband-wife relationships for all time.

We must continually remind ourselves that the Bible was written by human beings who were deeply influenced by the culture in which they found themselves, just as we are today. Naturally, the culture would affect the way in which they wrote about the revelations of God. It is indeed unfortunate that as we read the Bible we so often confuse the precepts of first-century Palestinian culture with absolute truth.

The Church has also used the Bible to oppress women by making special note that the Bible says Jesus chose only men for his closest disciples. Some denominations have long used this argument to deny women entrance to the ordained ministry or ordained priesthood. Let's look closer at this argument. First of all, it is true that Jesus did not choose any women to be a part of the inner circle of those nearest to him. What is the significance of that fact? It is commonly agreed that the twelve disciples "represented" the Twelve Tribes of Israel. It was also commonly understood that when the Messiah came he would reestablish the Twelve Tribes. Given the status of women in the Jewish religion, and the fact that ritually only males could be true Israelites in the fullest sense of the word, the symbolism of the Twelve Tribes would have been lost in the eyes of the Jewish community had women been included in the twelve. As to women being excluded from ministry because the twelve disciples were all male, it should be noted that the original apostles performed once and for all time the function of representing the Twelve Tribes of Israel. There is no reason to view the ordained minister of today as continuing that function. Women are not asking to be apostles, they are asking to be ministers. Of course, if one really insists that women should not be ordained because Jesus called no women, it should be pointed out that neither did Jesus call any Gentiles. Does that mean that only Jews should be ordained as Christian ministers?

Secondly, if Jesus had chosen women as a part of the twelve, they would have been subjected to an unnecessary amount of public ridicule by living so intimately with a group of men. In a time when women's relationships to men other than their husbands were minimal, it would have been most difficult for any women involved. Exposing women to that kind of ridicule and loss of reputation was never a part of Jesus' ministry.

However, it should be noted that women were indeed a part of the larger group of disciples which followed Jesus around the countryside. Some of them even helped to support Jesus' ministry financially. Luke reports that Jesus "went on through cities and villages, preaching and bringing the good news of the kingdom of God. And the twelve were with him, and also some women who had been healed of evil spirits and infirmities: Mary, called Magdalene, from whom seven demons had gone out; and Joanna, the wife of Chuza, Herod's steward; and Susanna; and many others, who provided for them out of their means" (Luke 8:1–3). So women were definitely a part of Jesus' public ministry even though they were not a part of the inner circle.

In fact, one of the main thrusts of Jesus' ministry and of the New Testament is the affirmation of the worth of women and their equality with men. Not once is there recorded an incident in Jesus' ministry nor any words of his which indicate that women are second to men in any way. To the contrary, his every relationship with women affirmed their dignity as persons equal with men in the sight of God. Of course, in order to do so Jesus had to break severely with the status quo which denied women such worth.

Many of us, reading the Gospels out of a twentieth-century background, are not aware of the tremendous significance of Jesus' actions toward women. For instance, it seems only natural that Jesus would talk with a woman at the well where he stopped for a drink of water. Once we become aware of the fact that rabbis (teachers) in that culture did not ordinarily speak with women in public, Jesus' action takes on new meaning. It was felt that a learned man such as a rabbi was simply wasting his time talking about religious concerns with women or indeed talking with them at all. Thus, there was a great deal of preju-dice against such conversations between the sexes. This particu-

lar story is often interpreted as indicating Jesus' lack of preju-
dice against Samaritans, but the remark made by the writer of
John indicates something else at work here. "Just then the disciples came. They marveled that he was talking with a *woman*
. . . (our italics, John 4:27). It should also be noted that Jesus was
not just passing the time of day with this woman; he was revealing for the first time that he was the expected Messiah. "The
woman said to him, 'I know that Messiah is coming (he who is
called Christ); when he comes, he will show us all things.' Jesus
said to her, 'I who speak to you am he' " (John 4:25, 26).

In a similar instance, in the home of his good friends Mary and
Martha, Jesus encouraged a woman to listen and converse with
him about spiritual matters. When Martha complained to Jesus
that Mary wasn't playing the traditional feminine role of preparing and serving food to the men, Jesus affirmed that Mary
was doing the right thing. "Martha, Martha, you are anxious and
troubled about many things; one thing is needful. Mary has
chosen the good portion, which shall not be taken away from
her" (Luke 10:38). Unfortunately, the church has not generally
paid much attention to this passage and has insisted that the
"proper" role for women in the church is not the intellectual
one but rather that of the housekeeper, thereby denying both
women and men the opportunity to choose how they will use
their own unique and God-given talents.

Still another incident from Jesus' ministry bears examination,
namely that a woman (or women) was the first witness to his
resurrection. Most Christians are so used to hearing the Easter
story that much of its impact concerning women is lost. While
we've grown accustomed to hearing how Jesus first appeared to
Mary Magdalene after the resurrection, we've missed the real
significance of this appearance. To make a woman the first
witness to such an extraordinary and significant event was totally unknown in Jesus' time. In fact, in the society of Jesus' day
the witness of women was not even acceptable in a court of law.

In spite of this, Jesus appeared first of all to a woman. Partly because of the extraordinariness of the event, but partly out of a lack of trust in the words of women, the men refused to believe them: "but these words seemed to them an idle tale, and they did not believe them" (Luke 24:11).

In the new order which Jesus is ushering in, women are to be given their rightful status and dignity as daughters of God, equal in every way to the sons of God. If in a fallen, unredeemed state women were seen as inferior to men: "yet your desire shall be for your husband, and he shall rule over you" (Genesis 3:16); now that the world has been redeemed through Jesus Christ, woman is to be restored to her rightful place as equal to man.

Nowhere is woman's status in this new order made more clear than in Paul's dramatic reversal of the old prayer of thanksgiving prayed daily by the Jewish males. Paul, being a devout Jew, no doubt prayed with his fellow Jews, "Praised be God that he has not created me a Gentile; praised be God that he has not created me a woman; praised be God that he has not created me an ignorant man" (or a slave). When Paul became a Christian, however, he said, "There is neither Jew nor Greek, there is neither slave nor free, there is neither male nor female; for you are all one in Christ Jesus" (Galatians 3:28). In Christ there is a new order of creation.

At various times in history the truth of Paul's statement has been seriously questioned, but out of the controversies came a greater appreciation of and affirmation of the truth it embodies. In the first century, one of the arguments revolved around the line, "There is neither Jew nor Greek." There were those who insisted that in order to be "in Christ" one must first become a Jew by submitting to circumcision. The essence of this position was to contend that there was indeed both Jew and Greek and that being a Jew was in some sense better than being a Greek since Jewishness was a prerequisite for becoming a Christian. In the nineteenth century the second line of that passage was severely tested by the Church as it struggled with the question of slavery, finally deciding that human slavery was inconsistent with the Christian faith. Now, in the twentieth century, it is our turn to struggle with the final line in that trilogy: "There is neither male nor female." What does that statement mean in relation to sexist worship? What does it say about the stereotyping of roles within the Church? About decision making at all levels of the Church? About the witness the Church makes to society in regard to women? About the seriousness or lack of seriousness with which the Church takes the liberation of women?

Is the Bible a stumbling block to women's liberation? We think not. It is our conviction that the overwhelming witness of the Bible, and the New Testament in particular, is a witness for the full personhood of all people, including women. Specifically, this also means a clear call for the elimination of sexist attitudes and traditions within the worship service. Sexist worship, as worship is usually conducted in most Christian churches today, goes against the teachings of Jesus. If we would follow Christ in treating women as whole persons, significant in the eyes of God, we must begin today to affirm the worth of women within the context of worship.

✤3✤

Freeing Our Concept
of God
from Sexism

GOD AS MOTHER. "Impossible!" you say? "Blasphemy!" "Sure, we call God "he" but I really don't think of God as a man, as being part of the male sex. After all, though, didn't Jesus himself call God "Father"?

What makes us so reluctant to think of God in feminine terms? Have masculinity and divinity become so bound up with each other that it is blasphemous to think of God as feminine?

Perhaps it would be helpful in dealing with this question to look first at why Jesus might have addressed God as "Father" and asked us to do the same. Jesus was trying to express that God loves all human beings, regardless of wealth, position, or status. One of the best metaphors to use in getting this idea across is the metaphor of the father who loves his children, and not merely tolerates them. In a patriarchal society such as the one in which Jesus lived, what better image could he use to indicate God's care and concern? By calling God "Father," Jesus was also saying that God is accessible; we should communicate with God in much the same way we communicate with another human being, such as our earthly father.

Finally, Jesus was saying that God is due the same kind of respect that children in a patriarchal society gave their father. None of these ideas is betrayed today, however, by calling God "Mother."

19

And Jesus himself did not deny the feminine within God. Quite the contrary. In telling the parable of the lost coin (Luke 15:8–10), Jesus cast a woman in the role of the God who searches and searches until the one lost coin (human being) is found. A simple story, perhaps, but one with profound ramifications. But most of us are so accustomed to thinking of God as a male that we don't even make the connection between God and the woman in this parable.

Let's go back now to the statement that calling God "he" doesn't mean we actually think of God as a male. How many times have you heard someone talk about God as "the *man* upstairs"? Why is it that when children are asked to describe God they almost always describe a *man,* usually complete with long white beard? Artists too have contributed to this idea. (Michelangelo, is a notorious example of one who used this kind of imagery, witness the Sistine Chapel.) Clearly, the mental picture of God that most of us get is one of a male being. And this mental picture profoundly influences our concept of God.

If "he," "him," and "his" when applied to God actually do not designate *maleness,* but rather are used "generically"—that is, to mean that God includes both male and female—then there should be no objection to using "she," "her," and "hers" in reference to God also. The fact that people do get upset or perhaps more frequently laugh, in the rare instances when God is called "she," indicates that our conception of God as strictly male is much more deeply entrenched than we will admit.

For all of their patriarchal ways, even the Jewish writers of the Old Testament did not always use masculine imagery to describe God. In Deuteronomy 32:18 (RSV) we find the words, "You were unmindful of the Rock that begot (or bore) you, and you forgot the God who gave you birth." Here is a passage which definitely pictures God as feminine. And again in Isaiah 42:14, "For a long time I have held my peace, I have kept still and restrained myself; Now I will cry out like a woman in travail. I will gasp and pant." What do we do with these passages? For too long the answer has been, "Ignore them." The time has come to take them seriously as we struggle to know God more fully. We need to hear these passages just as distinctly as those that speak of God's masculinity. Granted, there are not so many of these passages, but the fact that these words were sounded at all in a partiarchal religion and society is cause to take them seriously today.

But maybe you are thinking, "Why all the fuss? Can't we leave the time-tested concepts of God alone and just try to serve him (sic)?" There are at least two reasons why the answer to that question must be a resounding "No!"

First of all, an ever-increasing number of women is discovering that they feel a basic alienation from the masculine God of traditional Christianity at the very point of their sexuality. How can they, female human beings, identify themselves with a masculine God? When a woman tries to pattern herself after the highest and best that she knows, she discovers a deep schism which cuts her off from her God, a God who is totally other than she. Not only is there the basic difference between the Creator and the creature which all humans experience, but there is also the difference between male and female. This sense of otherness does not exist for most males, for when they look to God they experience a oneness with God at the point of their masculinity. In striving to be like Christ, they share with him not only the human experience but the masculine experience as well. For a woman there is no such shared identity, only the feeling of otherness, often alienation.

Secondly, and even more important, there is the firm conviction of growing numbers of women that God is trying to reveal another aspect of "himself" to us today. In the past we have recognized the masculine aspects of God. Now it is time to recognize God's feminine aspects as well. If God is revealing himself/herself to us, we must be willing to open our minds and hearts to that revelation.

It is noteworthy that while we have clung tenaciously to a

masculine "Father" God in the Christian church, we have nevertheless found subtle ways of attempting to incorporate the feminine within that masculine God. One of the most common of these attempts is to say "Mother Nature" when speaking of God's creative activity in the world. *"Mother Nature* dressed the trees in gorgeous autumn colors" means the same thing to many as saying that "God dressed the trees in gorgeous autumn colors." Somehow we can accept Mother Nature, but Mother God—that's another story!

God is often described as compassionate, kind, gentle, forgiving, loving, tender—qualities that have traditionally been assigned to the female sex rather than the male sex in our culture. The irony comes when we take these so-called "feminine" qualities and apply them to God. The God who possesses the "feminine" characteristics is then labeled "Father." We can picture God as being like our culture's ideal mother, but we refuse to admit what we are doing and we refuse consciously to see God as being in any way feminine. Is femininity so inferior to masculinity that we feel we would be showing God disrespect to apply to God the feminine labels such as "Mother" or "Queen"?

The Roman Catholic church has dealt with this need to recognize God's femininity and masculinity by elevating Mary's role as Virgin Mother to a position of divinity or near divinity. While this role has often been ridiculed by Protestants, it may be that such a theology comes nearer the truth than does the Protestant theology with its heavy masculine bias. It is interesting that today, when women are gaining in status and the idea of God as totally masculine is being challenged, Mary's prominence is declining. This is as it should be, for the need to divinize Mary disappears when God's own femininity is acknowledged and affirmed.

The masculinity of God has certainly been supported by the Incarnation in Jesus Christ, a male. We in no way deny the masculinity of Jesus, but we do deny the great significance which has been attached to his maleness by the Church. All of us are familiar with the pictures of the Nativity which show a Chinese holy family with a Chinese Christ child, an Indian Christ, a Spanish Christ, and so on. We do not get angry and upset and say, "That's not the way it was!" Instead, we affirm that Christ's Jewishness did not completely define him; that in a sense he belongs to all races, to all nationalities. Today in Africa and America there is an increasing emphasis on a black Christ. We know, of course, that Jesus was not black, but we can affirm that Christ belongs to the black race as much as to the white, the yellow, the brown, and the red.

Just as Christ was actually a Jew while here physically on earth, so he was also a male. We have recognized that Christ might have been born into any race, and indeed was born into every race in the deepest sense. Just as we have acknowledged that his Jewishness did not totally define Christ, can we not also acknowledge that neither is he totally defined by his maleness? As Christ "belongs" to all races and nationalities, can he not also belong to both sexes? We do not often speak of Jesus the *Jew*, but how often do we talk about the *man* Jesus! It is as though Christ cannot be separated from his maleness, but he can easily be separated from his Jewishness. There are many people who somehow accept the idea of a black Christ but not a female Christ. But are not Christ's skin color and his sex both of the same essence—incidental to his Christ-ness? If the society had been reversed and Palestine had been a matriarchy instead of a partiarchy, surely God would have sent her Daughter.

We are not saying that there should now be a dramatic switch in our concept of God and that whereas God in the past was considered masculine, from now on God shall be known as feminine. Not at all. To do that would be to gain absolutely nothing. What we are saying is that it is necessary that we perceive God as containing both the masculine and the feminine, as these qualities have traditionally been understood in our culture. And it is important to realize also that unlike maleness and femaleness, what is "masculine" and what is "feminine" is determined and defined not by nature but by our culture. Of course, God transcends maleness and femaleness since these are human categories. But as long as we have only human experiences and human terms with which to describe God, we will necessarily find ourselves applying human characteristics to God.

For nearly a century the Christian Scientists have spoken of God as both Father and Mother. The time has come for the Church as a whole to reexamine its theology of God and to become aware of the narrow-sightedness with which we have looked upon God. How can we truly call God "Father" if we cannot in the same breath say "Mother"?

While we may express our concept of the masculinity and femininity of God by saying Mother/Father, some find it desirable today to de-emphasize both the parent-figure within God and the "sexuality" of God by using terms other than Mother/Father, he/she. One problem that people encounter in thinking of God as Mother or Father or Parent is that their understanding of God is greatly influenced by their relationship with their own parents. A person who has not known a loving and trustworthy parent may find it impossible to trust a God whom she or he is encouraged to think of as Father or Mother.

That person may want to think of God as Creator or as Redeemer, titles which imply no gender. Thus, "Father, Son, and Holy Spirit" might become "Creator, Redeemer, and Sustainer" or "Creator, Savior, and Holy Spirit" or any number of such titles which in no way imply that God is a sexual being. One value of this approach is that it might help us to understand more clearly that God is Spirit and minimize our tendency to anthropomorphize God as "the man upstairs." As we come to affirm that God is Spirit, with qualities that we humans have sometimes understood as either masculine or feminine, we will be better able to worship God in spirit and in truth.

✤4✤

Hymnody Hangups

WE NOW MOVE into the action part of our book. You're convinced that we need to eliminate sexism in worship, but how do we do it? Especially, how do we do it when some of our worship resources are quite costly and not easily replaceable?

We're tackling hymns first because in many ways they seem the most difficult. Most churches mimeograph their own bulletins and therefore have control over the language of prayers, litanies, sermon titles, and so forth. But churches usually have invested considerable money in the hymnals they use each Sunday. As these books are already there, and filled with sexism, what can we do about them?

We've found three basic approaches helpful in dealing with hymns, whether traditional or folk in style. First, there are many good hymns in all the major denominational hymnals that are not sexist. You should analyze your hymnal and make a list of these hymns for your use. (Also see Appendix A.)

Second, many of the other hymns in the hymnals can be changed easily from sexist to non-sexist songs. This can be done by mimeographing the edited verses in the bulletin as part of the order of worship. Many churches are including the words to hymns in their bulletins now, anyway, so that they can increase the variety of hymns available to them. With the advent of Xerox, offset, and electronic stencils, churches now have the capability of inexpensively making their own mini-hymnals of non-copyrighted traditional and/or new original hymns. Don't overlook this possibility. In fact, many congregations come to prefer having everything, including the hymns, in their bulletins so that they don't have to juggle a hymnal along with the bulletin. In many sanctuaries it is also possible to project words and music onto a screen for all to see and use. Be sure to obtain permission to reproduce either the words or music or both of any copyrighted material. If you do not, you are opening yourself to suit by the copyright holder.

Third, encourage interested persons in your congregation to write new hymns either to old hymn tunes or folk tunes or to their own original music. When you encourage this creativity, also help the persons involved to see how important it is to avoid sexism in their creations. This creating of new hymns can bring great excitement and meaning to a congregation's worship, as well as give tremendous satisfaction to the persons who do the creating.

Let's go back to these three basic methods of handling sexism in hymns and explore each in more detail. Which method or combination of methods you use will depend a great deal on your particular congregation and your particular resources.

Choosing non-sexist hymns from the hymnal your congregation uses regularly should probably be your first step. Of course, if you are already using many different hymnals, or if you mimeograph your hymns onto your bulletins, the first step won't be quite so important. On the other hand if your congregation has been singing from only one hymnal, switching too suddenly to another style might prove upsetting to many people. Generally, a better method for introducing change in worship is to do it gradually, after a great deal of careful explanation is made as to why it is being done. We have included a list of fifty fairly well-known non-sexist hymns in the appendix to this book. You can take this as a beginning, but do take the time to go through your own church's hymnal and list all the hymns that are non-sexist. Such a list will save you time in choosing

hymns, as you will not have to re-read every hymn for each
worship service. Chances are you may discover some great
hymns you haven't used all that much. If you are a lay person
in your church, take the list you've made to your pastor and
explain to him or her why you feel it is important to use non-
sexist hymns. You may want to give your pastor a copy of this
book, if he or she doesn't already have it. If your church is using
one hymnal exclusively, you will also want to consider gradually
opening up your congregation to the use of other hymns and/or
hymnals as supplementary resources. Often the best way to do
this is to pick a hymn that you know many persons in your
congregation really like but that is not in the hymnal you regularly use. Such a strategy helps most of your congregation to
approach the idea of using supplementary hymns favorably,
and then you can introduce new unfamiliar hymns much more
easily later.

When you have succeeded in increasing the understanding of
a large number of persons in your congregation to the problem
of sexism, you will be ready to move to the second method of
dealing with sexist hymns, i.e., editing hymns that have certain
sexist words. Sometimes this is a relatively simple job. Other
times it can be quite difficult, because of the need for matching
not just meanings but also syllables and sometimes rhyme and
rhythms.

We've found that the more we do this kind of editing, the
easier it gets. We discover words that seem to substitute well for
others and methods of changing particular lines of hymns while
still maintaining the right syllables and rhymes. Each hymn has
to be treated individually, however, because there are often
quite different meanings intended by use of the same word.
Each hymn must thus be edited within its own context, and no
absolute rules for editing all hymns can be laid down. However,
it is possible to share with you some of the methods of editing
we have found helpful and which will make your job easier.

We've discovered that sometimes editing not only eliminates the sexism in a particular hymn, but also gives that hymn a deepened meaning.

A good word to substitute for "men" is "folk." "Folk" implies the common people. It has an element of friendliness and unity to it which really makes it a better choice for many songs where "men" is used. For example, the song "Rise Up, O Men of God" takes on a new and deeper meaning when it is changed to "Rise Up, O Folk of God." The same is true with "Good Christian Men (Folk), Rejoice and Sing." Another solution to this problem is to substitute the first person plural ("we" or "us") for "men" or "man." Thus, the line "Born that man no more may die" from "Hark the Herald Angels Sing" could be sung "Born that we no more may die." Using the first person "we" also tends to make the words more immediate and personal than the more formal and impersonal "man."

It is often possible to substitute the word "one" for the singular "man." Thus, in the contemporary folk hymn "They'll Know We Are Christians by Our Love," the sexism that appears in the third verse can be easily eliminated by substituting: "We'll guard each man's (one's) dignity and save each man's (one's) pride." It is also possible to substitute the word "human" or "person" for the word "man." This often requires a rearranging of some other words in the hymn so that the syllables will come out right, but it can be done. Thus the contemporary folk hymn "Morningsong," which appears in *Hymns for Now III*, has one line that reads "Hopeless seems the time of man with desolation near." This can be rearranged to eliminate the sexism by saying "Hopeless seems our human time with desolation near."

The word "Parent" can almost always be substituted for the word "Father." Thus, "God of Our Fathers" becomes "God of Our Parents." "Brightly Beams Our Father's Mercy" becomes "Brightly Beams Our Parent's Mercy."

It is important, however, to be sensitive to the readiness of your own congregation to accept such language changes. Most congregations will be able to accept the substitution of "parent" for "father" quite readily when it refers generically to human fathers. When it refers to God the Father, such acceptance will not come so quickly. Before making such a substitution you should spend a little time educating your congregation about Jesus' use of the word "Father" and why that word today should more appropriately be rendered "Parent."

There is a logical substitution for "brotherhood," but it is so seldom used that it too will take real preparation of your congregation before it can be meaningfully introduced. The word is "siblinghood." Our problem with this word is that right now it does not have nearly the feeling tone of "brotherhood." The word "sibling" has been associated by most of us with academic or clinical settings. It has none of the warmth and emotive power of "brother" or "sister." Thus, you must decide either to try to help persons invest new warmth in that word or try to develop other ways of editing out "brotherhood," such as adding the word "sisterhood" when this is possible or the word "friends" even though this word, too, is not as strong emotively as "brotherhood." Thus, the line in the fourth verse of the contemporary folk hymn "Clap Your Hands" can be changed from "Those who want to live in peace and brotherhood," to "Those who want to live in peace and friendship." Other possibilities for that line are "Those who want to live in peace and harmony."

It is also hard to find a non-sexist equivalent for the word "brother" that will be the same number of syllables. "Neighbor" sometimes works well. Thus, the contemporary folk hymn "Brothers, Get Yourselves Together," can be changed to "Neighbors, Get Yourselves Together." Sometimes it is also possible to substitute the word "other" for "brother."

As with "brother," so with "son" and "sons," it is difficult to find a good equivalent. Sometimes it may be possible to reword the song and say "sons and daughters." Usually, however, it is necessary to find a one syllable substitute for the word. Here again the word "folk" is handy. Thus "Sons of God" becomes "Folk of God."

The word "mankind" can perhaps best be replaced by the words "humans" or "people." Thus, in "All You People Clap Your Hands," the line in the chorus that reads "The Lord has made all mankind one" can be changed to "Our God has made all humans (people) one."

In hymnody and liturgy the Church is often referred to as "she," as well as are inanimate objects in common speech. People will often apply the feminine pronoun "she" or "her" to things such as cars, ships, planes, and so on. Many women find it demeaning to be classed in the same category as "things," realizing that the masculine pronouns "he," "him," and "his" are reserved for human beings alone. When speaking of a genderless object such as a car or a genderless institution such as the Church it is appropriate, and for many women essential to use the neuter pronoun "it" rather than the feminine "she."

Many people have asked us about the word "Amen." "Is that not a sexist term?" they wonder. Actually no, since "Amen" is a Hebrew word meaning "So be it" and has nothing whatever to do with men. However, you might find it more meaningful occasionally to substitute "So be it" for "Amen" at the conclusion of hymns and prayers. "Alleluia" or "Hallelujah" meaning "Praise God" in Greek and Hebrew respectively might also be substituted. And, of course, the current phrase "Right on!" will speak to some people more clearly than "Amen."

After you have had a chance to educate a significant segment of your church to the evils of sexism in hymns, you may want to get a group together to edit your hymnals by hand. This takes a great deal of person power, but if the interested people are readily available the editing can be done fairly quickly. You may want to start just with some of your congregation's favorite sexist hymns. There is no sense spending a lot of time editing something no one will ever use.

If your church is already using a bulletin in which even the hymns are reproduced, your job should be somewhat easier. However, if you plan to reproduce both words and music to a contemporary copyrighted hymn you must obtain permission to do so. To reproduce copyrighted material without permission is a form of stealing. And yet it is almost impossible to get permission quickly to reproduce all the different hymns you'll want to use. Some people solve this problem by using increasing numbers of hymns their own congregation has written. Others rewrite their hymns so completely they feel they have created a new composition. Hopefully more music companies will follow the lead of F.E.L. Publishing House and provide a loose-leaf hymnal service so that churches may purchase copies of single hymns cheaply. This means the church doesn't have to worry about a lot of printing hassle. It also means that the hymn writers receive the royalties due them. Hopefully, in the future, song publishers, especially including those who have published the various denominational hymnals, will begin offering this loose-leaf service, not only to provide churches with good new hymns but also to provide them with edited new versions of former sexist hymns.

One of the best ways to accomplish the third suggestion for obtaining non-sexist hymns—that is have persons in your congregation write new original hymns—is to have periodic hymn-composing workshops. Whoever leads such sessions should be sure that the persons involved clearly know what sexisms in hymns are and why they are so damaging. Perhaps sections of Chapter 1 from this book could be discussed with them so they could begin to understand what such sexisms do to an increasing number of women. These workshops do not necessarily need to be large—two or three persons who have a gift in this area can be tremendously valuable in providing many fresh hymns for your congregation.

Finally, it is important to note that no amount of editing will eliminate the sexism from some verses of some hymns. The folk hymn, "Well, It's a New Day" has a verse that says "A sinful man lusts for power and fame, Women, wealth, and wine, But there's a New Law, there's a New Law: A man can lust in his mind." The only valid way to use that hymn if it must be used, is to have only men sing that particular verse. Then the use of the word "man" will be interpreted non-generically all the way through.

Hymns are powerful instruments of our faith. When all else about a service is forgotten we may still be humming or singing lines from one of the hymns. Because of their sustaining power, it is especially important that we begin work to eliminate sexism in hymns immediately.

❖5❖

Liberating the Liturgy

THERE ARE TWO major aspects of the liturgy that need to be liberated—its language and its leadership.

All that we said concerning changing language in our chapter on hymns applies here, too, except that it is often not so necessary to match up syllable, rhyme, and rhythm. Therefore, it is usually not difficult to take each part of your liturgical language and edit out the sexism. In addition to editing old prayers and responses, you should be open to the tremendous possibilities of using new prayers and responses. Examples of such contemporary elements of liturgy are presented in the next chapter. We hope they are enough to get you started. The more persons in your congregation that you can get to help write new prayers and responses, the more your liturgy will truly become the work of the people. Many churches now have liturgy committees which meet weekly to develop the worship service for the coming Sunday. People on these committees are rotated so that many persons in a congregation have an opportunity to experience helping to create a worship service.

One question that is often asked when we talk about liberating the language of worship is "What about sexist language found in the Bible—do we have the right to edit that?" Some people feel that any "tampering" with the Bible is anathema and reject out of hand any possibility for editing out sexist language. They forget that the Bibles they are using are themselves translations of early manuscripts which do not always agree.* But even if we had the original manuscripts of the Old and New Testaments and an agreed upon, or literal, translation, undoubtedly there would continue to be much sexist language in the Bible. After all, it does reflect the highly patriarchal climate in which it was written.

Some persons feel we should leave this language as is, recognizing that the Bible was written in a particular historical period and is bound to reflect some of the culture and language of that period. These persons point out that the amazing thing about the New Testament is not that it contains some sexist language, but that it so often and so clearly sees women in a new equality with men. They also point out that if we justify editing out the sexism in our Bibles, some other group will want to edit out something else, and pretty soon some of the eternal validity of the Bible will be erased by groups who have modernized it on this issue and that.

Such an argument appears wise at first blush. Certainly we must be careful not to change the Bible. A study of Church history quickly teaches us that what one generation doesn't understand or finds objectionable in the Bible, other generations find meaningful. If we begin editing the Bible to meet our own tastes, we will weaken its power to confront us with words we may not wish to hear.

But to eliminate the sexist language of the Bible is, as we see it, much more in the realm of a contemporary translation or amplification, such as the work of J. B. Phillips, than it is changing the Bible. The job of a translator is to try to put the words and meanings of the original writers in contemporary and understandable language. For instance, where the words "man"** or

*For an interesting treatment of the way male translators of the biblical texts have shown their male bias, see the article by Ruth Hoppin listed in the resource section of this book.

**The word generally translated "man" in English is actually the Greek word for "human being."

"sons" are used generically they ought to be translated for our contemporary society into their full meaning, such as "human" or "sons and daughters." This is not changing the real meaning of the words or even editing out large sections of the Bible, but instead is amplifying the meaning of the original words.

Our problem is that as of now no version of the Bible has done this. The one that we have found often coming the closest is *The New English Bible*. Even this translation, however, has much needless sexist language. What we, the authors, are doing until a non-sexist version of the Bible is produced is simply inserting the appropriate changes as we read. We do this in our imaginations as we read passages for our own study and meditation, and we do it also as we read the Scripture in worship. We encourage others who read Scripture during worship to do the same.

Liberating the leadership in worship services may prove to be an even more difficult task than freeing its language. Because the overwhelming majority of ministers are men, liturgy leadership is already dangerously overbalanced. Protestant seminaries all over the country, however, are reporting record enrollments of women in their programs for ordination, so this overbalance may correct itself, at least partially, in a few years. Until then, it will be doubly important to have lay persons involved in the leadership of worship, and in most cases these lay persons should be women, to balance the male clergy.

Many churches already have lay persons assist with the worship services. If your church does not do this, you will want to help it begin this practice. Such leadership makes sense theologically—worship is a congregation's theology acted out and certainly lay representatives of the congregation should be involved in the leadership of this experience. Unfortunately, even those churches which have used lay leadership have most often used men rather than women. This is especially true of large prestigious churches.

How do you go about balancing the liturgical leadership in your own church? If you are the pastor of a local church, you can simply choose persons of the opposite sex to help you lead the liturgy. It's certainly permissible to choose more than one. Thus, if you are a man, you might choose two women and a man to help you in some services, only one woman in others. The important thing is that balance in leadership be maintained. If you are a lay person, you will have to try to convince your pastor that this balance is important. Some of the discussion in Chapter 1 of this book might be helpful here. Make sure your pastor realizes that the majority of persons attending churches across the country are women, and that they are often totally left out of the worship leadership. When you have talked with your pastor, don't be satisfied with an occasional token woman as worship leader. If your pastor is male, ask him how he would feel if most of the persons in the congregation were male but only occasionally did a male ever participate in worship leadership.

One of the problems you may face as you attempt to affect a balance of worship leadership is the response from many women that they don't want to be leaders because they get frightened before a group. This comes from men, too, but not so often. This is a very real fear, and it should not be treated lightly. Often it comes out of deep feelings of inferiority that have been pressed upon women for many years. Because of these feelings some women may not want to lead in worship services. We must respect their feelings at this point and not attempt to pressure them into something they don't wish to do. Other women can be found who will want to provide such leadership. What may help women to want to lead in worship is to provide a training course for worship leaders. At one church we served, all lay worship leaders were required to take a special six-week training course. This dealt with theology and worship, but it also dealt with practical matters such as speaking before a group, using a microphone, reading Scripture with meaning, and so forth. We found this to be one of our most fruitful adult education experiences. We also found that it gave a new confidence to persons who were fearful when standing before an audience. In addition, we found that as women become accustomed to seeing other women leading worship, they often gain confidence in their own ability to be worship leaders.

Another possible problem in extending liturgical leadership to women is the condescending attitude that is often conveyed by male ministers. Such phrases as "the lovely ladies" or "what would our church do without its wonderful women's societies" often betray a view of women as almost children, to be cajoled, patted on the head, tolerated in a benign way. It is extremely important that such an attitude be confronted and changed. The most perfectly balanced liturgical leadership with the best non-sexist language in hymns, prayers, and responses can still be torpedoed by such an attitude. Again the only way we know to handle this is through education and sometimes through gentle but firm pressure. As it is often unconscious behavior, so the first step then may be helping the pastor become aware of what he is doing.

When we speak of liberating the liturgy, we must also see the possibilities for bringing greater variety in dress and tone. Women involved in leading worship should not have to wear the black scholar's robe that many male ministers still wear. They should be encouraged to use their imaginations to come up with new and more appropriate liturgical garb. If they do this, the men who lead in worship, both clerical and lay, may see new possibilities for their own liturgical dress. We have found liturgical ponchos quite effective, for example. They can be made out of homespun or cotton and then liturgical symbols for the various seasons of the church year, or for particular services, can be embroidered or sewn on. We usually use a white material on which various colored symbols are sewn. All different colors of liturgical garb are appropriate, however, and if worship leaders begin using more colors, this may help lift the drabness from many services.

Not only is it important to make sure that sexism is eliminated from both the language of the liturgy and from its leadership, it is also essential that even small details connected with the service reflect the equality of the sexes. Perhaps this is nowhere more true than in the listing of names in the worship bulletin. For many years in most organizations it has been customary to list married women in relation to their husbands. Thus, listings of officers in the women's society of a church often read like this: Mrs. Harold Jones, president; Mrs. John Rider, vice-president, and so on. This manner of listing names only serves to perpetuate the myth that women gain their identity and their importance through men. It implies that a married woman is simply an appendage of her husband as well as implying ownership of the wife by the husband. It has often been said that "in marriage the two become one and that one is the husband." The most blatant example of that kind of fallacious thinking is shown by referring to a husband and wife as "the Steven Johnsons."

Further, the traditional titles of Miss and Mrs. seem to be saying that for a woman the most important identifying characteristic is whether or not she is attached to a man by means of marriage. In common practice titles are often used with women's names while they are not with men's names. Names in a bulletin thus appear as follows: James Olsen, Mrs. Philip Carter, Miss Grace Thompson, Richard Henderson. . . . One can only assume that the reason the titles are necessary for women but unnecessary for men is to indicate the woman's relationship or lack of relationship to a man.

Perhaps the best way to deal with this problem is simply to eliminate the use of titles. In the Church, where we claim to be "brothers and sisters in Christ," why should we address each other as "Mr." or "Mrs."? Would it not be better to use our

"Christian names" in addressing one another, as we do the brothers and sisters in our own families?

If titles must be used, the corresponding title to "Mr." should be "Ms." and not "Mrs." or "Miss." If a woman insists on being called Mrs. Husband's Name, that is her right, but such designation should certainly not be encouraged.

Some women object to the title "Ms." because they do not want to risk disapproval by society and by males, in particular, by identifying themselves in any way with the women's liberation movement. Others prefer to be called Mrs. Husband's Name simply because that has been the custom in which they grew up. They will say that "Ms." is all right for younger women but not for themselves. However, the issue at stake here is not what custom one feels comfortable with, but whether naming and identifying women in relation to men is demeaning to women. More and more women are deciding that it definitely is demeaning and that such a custom denies the full personhood of women.

Liberating the liturgy is not an easy task. People often resist tenaciously any changes in what they consider to be treasured ritual. Many pastors become accustomed to a particular style of leadership and they are not eager to change it. Do not become discouraged. Be willing to go slowly and accomplish your victory piecemeal. But do not give up or be fooled into thinking that no movement is slow movement. Change can and will come. The last chapter of this book gives some more detailed strategy that may be helpful to you when you find persons both in leadership and in the congregation resisting such change.

✤6✤

Liberated Prayers,
Affirmations,
and Responses

THE EDITING SUGGESTIONS MADE in Chapters 4 and 5 should also help you in rewriting prayers and responses, both traditional and contemporary. But you may feel a special need for more contemporary non-sexist liturgical expressions. There has been an abundance of contemporary worship resources produced in the last several years. Unfortunately, we know of none that is totally non-sexist. In fact, many of the so-called modern worship resources are more sexist than some older liturgical expressions. This is true because many modern liturgies stress our social responsibilities and our relationship to one another (with words such as brother and mankind used in abundance), whereas older liturgies tended to emphasize one's personal relationship to God. Therefore, we offer you a beginning selection of truly contemporary resources. These are intended to be only examples of what can be done. We hope you'll take them as such and develop your own creative liturgical resources from them.

You will note that in many of the prayers and responses we simply repeat the word God whenever it is used rather than attempting a pronoun such as he/she or rather than using a new term such as "parent." We feel that at the beginning of change in worship the use of God repeated when necessary rather than some new way of speaking of God will be less jarring to persons who are worshipping. As education concerning the concept of God progresses, it will be natural to refer to God with combined pronouns and with words such as "parent."

In this chapter we have divided the resources according to the basic parts of most worship services. (We realize that not all worship services use all the categories we will show and that others undoubtedly have additional ones.) You will discover too as you read through this section, that some of what is written can be adapted to other portions of your worship service. Don't hesitate to take what you feel is most meaningful to you and adapt it to be more useful to you.

The prayers and responses in this chapter are original with us in one sense, but dependent upon many others in another sense. As far as we know, we have originated or contributed to the particular wording in all these liturgical resources, but we realize that we have been affected by thousands of worship services we have experienced over many years. Often there are phrases and prayers in these services that have remained with us and become a part of who we both are. Usually, no credit is given on bulletins as to where a particular prayer or response has been obtained. In a sense we feel this is good because it helps to show the anonymous creative community throughout Christendom that is sharing without thought of personal credit what to them has been a most meaningful and significant response to God. We are sure we have been influenced more than we know by this great creative community. So if you read a phrase or paragraph that sounds much like something you have seen elsewhere, you probably have seen it somewhere else. This is our proclamation of thanks to all those creative persons who have helped us as we try to develop the most meaningful liturgical resources possible.

One further comment is important here. We think that most contemporary worship resources are far too wordy. Because words in worship are so important, we believe they should be used with economy. We feel that in many contemporary services so great an attempt has been made to include every idea that nothing is said well enough to be remembered. Words are fragile and delicate instruments and when they are piled on top of each other, especially in things that congregations are to read together, they tend to become meaningless and boring. Some of the most meaningful services we have experienced have been completely non-verbal communion services. Our society is beginning again also to recognize the tremendous value of silence, the universal language. So as you develop your own liturgical resources, remember to hold your words reverently and use them sparingly.

CALLS TO WORSHIP

LEADER: In the beginning there was the energy of creation . . . and it moved. And God said,—"Light!"

CONGREGATION: *And there IS light. And the energy continued to move . . . and God said, "Space!"*

LEADER: And there IS space. And the energy continued to move . . . and God said, "Earth!"

CONGREGATION: *And there IS earth. And the energy kept moving . . . and God said, "Male and Female!"*

LEADER: And there IS male and female . . . and we are here. And now the earth is ours to inherit, and the gifts of the earth.

CONGREGATION: *And so we come to worship to celebrate these gifts and to learn again what it means to be entrusted with them.*

✦ ✦ ✦

LEADER: Why are we gathered at this time and place?

CONGREGATION: *We are gathered as the people of God—to hold before us the mirror of the world, and the mirror that is Jesus Christ our Savior. And with these mirrors to see ourselves as we are and should be.*

LEADER: Then let us praise the Christ of us all—before whom we eternally stand.

✦ ✦ ✦

LEADER: Welcome in the name of the One who was no stranger to sorrow and who knew death so that we might more fully know life.

+ + +

CONGREGATION: We are children of God. We stand in communion with all persons everywhere. We come to this place today to hear again of God's fantastic love that calls us to a transforming care that literally reaches 'round the world.

+ + +

LEADER: Good morning!

CONGREGATION: *Good Morning!*

LEADER: Let us come together in the spirit of the One who unites us all;

CONGREGATION: *In the spirit of our Savior, Jesus Christ.*

LEADER: Let us remember that we are God's chosen people;

CONGREGATION: *Chosen to be God's servants in the world.*

LEADER: We gather because of our common need for renewal.

CONGREGATION: *Let us offer acceptable worship to God who renews us for service. Amen.*

+ + +

LEADER: We come together to thank the Creator of life.

CONGREGATION: *We come to praise God's holy name and to seek after God's ways.*

LEADER: We come to be forgiven and to forgive.

CONGREGATION: *We come to be a community in God's love.*

LEADER: We come, in short, to worship.

CONGREGATION: *Praise God.*

✦ ✦ ✦

LEADER: "I am the door. Come in. Do not be afraid." This is what Jesus says to those who stand half-secure behind half-shut doors.

CONGREGATION: *This is Jesus' saying to all the children of the earth who cling to their blankets of sin like silent crutches.*

LEADER: There are those moments when in the name of Jesus bold and certain people on earth must say: "Come in. Do not be afraid. It is I."

CONGREGATION: *Christ waits. There is room for all to come in, even through the half-open door. Sister and brother, come now. Come and learn and live.*

✦ ✦ ✦

LEADER: Now is the time to live: to come to the God who creates us, to sing to the Redeemer who frees us.

CONGREGATION: *Now is the time to come alive, to invite the whole world to join in praising God.*

LEADER: Yes, now is the time to invite the sky to thunder God's word, the earth to rumble in praise.

CONGREGATION: *We invite all to celebrate with us, to glorify God's name, to dance with God's Spirit, which fills us.*

✦ ✦ ✦

LEADER: To worship is to heighten our awareness of the poetry of our existence.

CONGREGATION: *It is to open all the windows of our being to the indwelling power of God's love.*

LEADER: It is to join the mighty chorus of praise and thanksgiving that has boomed out since the beginning of creation.

CONGREGATION: *To worship is joy. It's great to be here!*

✦ ✦ ✦

LEADER: "Behold, I stand at the door and knock. . . ."

CONGREGATION: *And what is that supposed to mean?*

LEADER: It's a way of saying that God is always seeking us.

CONGREGATION: *But has God found us?*

LEADER: God only fully finds us when we want to open ourselves to God's love. God does not force us, we must respond.

CONGREGATION: *The first step, then, is from God, and the response is our responsibility?*

LEADER: Right! And that's what worship is all about. Through worship we open doors through which the Spirit of God may move, and we can respond.

✦ ✦ ✦

LEADER: Why did you come here this morning?

CONGREGATION: *To find God.*

LEADER: I didn't know God was lost.

CONGREGATION: *God is lost so often in the busy routine of our daily lives. We come here today to open our lives to the invasion of God's life.*

LEADER: Well, let's get busy!

INVOCATIONS AND COLLECTS

Invocations

God, you're here, waiting for us. Before we ever thought of trying to find you, you came out to meet us. We're entering a treasured ritual now. It may be out of habit. It may be that someone forced us to come here. It may be that we are hungry or wistful. For whatever reason, we are here. Capture our minds and hearts and wills, so that we may worship you honestly and meet you truly. In the spirit of Christ. So be it.

✦ ✦ ✦

God, may the presence of your Holy Spirit, which is everywhere, be especially here now comforting us but also confronting us with the responsibility to make your word of love become flesh in our actions today. Amen.

✦ ✦ ✦

Amazing God, may the presence of your Holy Spirit descend upon your Church once more, awakening us and filling us with love and joy and power till Christ's love is alive in every human heart. Amen.

✦ ✦ ✦

LEADER: Come Holy Spirit!

CONGREGATION: *Inspire us in this hour of worship.*

LEADER. Inspire us so that we can breathe new life into old dreams.

CONGREGATION: *So that we can lose ourselves to find ourselves.*

LEADER: So that we can love without counting the cost.

CONGREGATION: *Come, Holy Spirit!*

✦ ✦ ✦

God, it almost seems presumptuous for us to ask you to be here with us. We know you're here already. But we also know that often we don't bother to be aware of your presence. Make us aware now in this time we've set aside for special sensitivity to you. Help us to be open to you and through you to others. Amen.

✦ ✦ ✦

God, may the presence of your Holy Spirit bring us alive inside to the wonder of love that reveals you everywhere. Amen.

✦ ✦ ✦

LEADER: God, we know that your Spirit hovers over us like a big bird.

CONGREGATION: *Help us to see your bright wings.*

LEADER: Help us to hear the cooing of your love in our own lives and all over the world.

CONGREGATION: *Help us to feel the warmth of your presence.*

LEADER: Help us to be the winged presence of your love to each other.

CONGREGATION: *Now and forever. Alleluia!*

✦ ✦ ✦

God, you're here waiting for us. Help us in this hour to wait for you. In our waiting help us to discover that life is never all it should be or can be and that expectation is essential to discovering new possibilities for your presence in us. Amen.

Collects

God, who comes to us in our great joys, our crushing sorrows, and in all the everydayness in between, be with us now as we share ourselves with one another in this time of worship. In Jesus' name we pray. Amen.

✦ ✦ ✦

Amazing God, whose glory outshines the sun, open our lives to the inspiration of your Holy Spirit that we may more fully reflect the glory of your love. In Christ's name we pray. Amen.

✦ ✦ ✦

God, who split the veil of the Holy of Holies when Jesus was raised, rip the veils from our hearts this day so that we may come alive to your love for us and for all persons. Alleluia!

✦ ✦ ✦

God, whose love is revealed in the tenderness of a mother's smile, help us to reflect the miracle of your tenderness and gentleness in our lives today. In Jesus' name we pray. Amen.

✦ ✦ ✦

God, who brought light from darkness, help us to see your light so well that it not only illumines our path but reflects off us to illumine others. We pray this prayer in the name of the One who was called the light of the world. Amen.

✦ ✦ ✦

God, who gave us the miracle of music, help us to bring our lives in tune with your will so well that true harmony can reign on earth. In Christ's name we pray, Amen.

✦ ✦ ✦

God, who died out on evil rather than striking back at it, help us to see the futility of force and violence as principles for our own lives or for our nation. We pray this prayer in the name of the One who gave his life for peace. Amen.

✦ ✦ ✦

God, who burst open Jesus' tomb, break open the tombs of indifference and despair that trap our lives. In Christ's name we pray, Amen.

✦ ✦ ✦

God, whose arms reach around all the griefs of the ages, be with us today and help us with the particular griefs that invade each of our lives. In Jesus' name we pray, Amen.

✦ ✦ ✦

God—who loves all people as a mother loves her children, not just because they are good but simply because they are—show us the way to love all your children as our sisters and brothers, simply because they are human. Amen.

✦ ✦ ✦

O God, in whom we were conceived and given birth, give us now the rocklike strength to stand firm in our commitment to you when others chase after false gods. Amen.

CONFESSION

Calls
Prayers
Words of Assurance

Calls to Confession

There is something wrong in us and around us. Let us admit it.

Christ is a mirror revealing to us how far we have fallen short of God's perfect love. We must admit our failures before God for this is the only way we can receive new strength to live more effectively.

We know better than we do. Let us confess the failures of our love and the confusion of our lives.

Let us confess honestly before God the things that we have done or failed to do which have caused us to be less effective servants.

We would like to look at ourselves and be wholly pleased with what we see. But the Christian gospel calls us to be honest. It forces us to be realistic. Let us, then, make a bold recognition that we are not pleased with what we see.

General Prayers of Confession
(Prayed by all)

O God, we admit that too often we live on the surface of life.
We are afraid of the depths, though we try to hide many things
deep within us. We are haunted by the knowledge that we have
hurt others by our own selfish acts. We are harassed by the
realization that our sense of priorities and laziness has pre-
vented us from responding to situations where we might have
made a creative difference. What gets into us God to make us
miss the mark of our Christian love time after time? Help us,
O God, we pray. Amen.

✦ ✦ ✦

LEADER: Let us confess our sin and admit who we are.

   Left: *We are impatient and bored.*

   Right: *We are often undisciplined and irresponsible.*

COMMUNITY: *Yeah, Jesus. . . . That's the way it is.*

   Left: *We care about the poor and the oppressed.*

   Right: *And we also care about cool buildings, comfortable
   chairs, color TV, and three good meals a day.*

COMMUNITY: *Yeah, Jesus. . . . That's the way it is.*

   Left: *We are not sensitive enough of others.*

   Right: *And too sensitive of ourselves.*

COMMUNITY: *Yeah, Jesus. . . . That's the way it is.*

✦ ✦ ✦

God, we come before you knowing we have tried to hide from
you, from one another, and from ourselves. Somehow we have

felt that by depending upon our own powers we could solve the problems of life. We have tried to escape by withdrawing from the difficult, the challenging, the crucifying experiences of life. We have become trapped in a meaningless round of insignificant activities while we have avoided projects we should have done. We have strayed far from the fullness of life you have promised us. Forgive us for our self-centeredness, our proudness, our weakness, our blindness. Have mercy upon us, that we may become your people anew. So be it.

God, we confess that we are frightened and humbled by the violence and hatred that we see rampant in our society and feel sometimes in ourselves. Forgive us for our lack of understanding and love. Help us to bear up under hatred and persecution and courageously stand for peace and justice. In Christ's name we pray, Amen.

O God, we admit that too often we see our lives as a burden to be borne rather than as a joy to be celebrated. Forgive us for getting bogged down in all our problems and heartaches. Help us to realize the joyous miracle of your love, even in the midst of discouragement and despair. In Christ's name we pray, Amen.

God, we turn to you to get the inside track and obtain special favors. We ask for your direction in our lives only when it coincides with the direction we want to go. We want your power only when it will help us with our own pet projects. We ask for your sanction for our ambitions. We want you to give us a blank check that we can fill out however we wish. Help us listen for what is your will for our lives. Help us be open to being

used by you rather than trying to use you. In Christ's name we
pray, Amen.

Mother and Father God, we know how often our world is torn
by hatred and misunderstanding, and we know how much this
pains you. We know that we are not personally responsible for
all of this tornness, but we also know we stand guilty for some
of it. There have been times when we have been quick to
accuse and slow to forgive. There have been times when we
have let small differences mushroom into vast difficulties while
at the same time we ignore important understandings that
should be drawing us together in love. For our tendency to push
hate before love and angry accusation before patient understanding, forgive us God. In Christ's name we pray, Amen.

God, forgive us for being asleep so often when you need us. You
writhe in the agony of the world's hungry while we worry over
whether to have steak or chicken tonight. You weep with the
soul of a person who is friendless while we fret over who to
invite to some social occasion. Wake us up to the needs of our
brothers and sisters everywhere. In Christ's name we pray,
Amen.

I'm sorry for the times someone wasn't beautiful
        and I looked away.
I'm sorry for the times someone stretched out a hand
        and I pretended not to notice.
I'm sorry for the times someone needed to be held
        and I clung to safety instead.
I'm sorry for the times truth was on my tongue
        and I swallowed it instead of speaking it.

I'm sorry for the times I satisfied my own desires
    and hurt someone else by my selfishness,

I'm sorry for the times love was in my heart
   and I was too embarrassed to express it.
I'm sorry for the times fear was in my heart
   and I didn't trust you with it.
I'm sorry for the times I claimed to be an innocent bystander
   and still I knew that by being a passive participant I was
   guilty for allowing wrong to be done.
I'm sorry for the times a stranger asked me for something
   and I pretended not to realize what he needed.
I'm sorry for the times I haven't loved enough
   and the times I haven't loved with all of me.
I know you know I'm sorry, God,
   and I know you've already forgiven me.
Maybe that's why I'm not ashamed to be sorry.

Father and Mother God, we confess that often we do not like
the bodies we have. Sometimes we long for different families.
We would exchange our jobs for the jobs of others. We would
like to do away with parts of our history. We are afraid of our
moods and feelings. We wish we had more time. We would like
to start over again. We lust after the prestige of others. We think
more money will solve our problems. We resent the injustices
we have suffered and cherish our sorrows. We want to be ap-
preciated for our small graces. We are enchanted by the past
and enticed by the future. We have never really been understood. In short, we have refused to live because we have held
out for better terms. Heal us, God, from the distance we have
tried to put between ourselves and life. Restore to us a love for
you and for all your creation. Help us be renewed in our whole
lives through Jesus Christ our Savior. Amen.

Words of Assurance

LEADER: There is no sin so terrible that God's love cannot forgive. In the name of Jesus Christ your sins are forgiven.

CONGREGATION: *There is no sin so terrible that God's love cannot forgive. In the name of Jesus Christ your sins are forgiven.*

✦ ✦ ✦

"The mercy of God is everlasting." Such is the witness of our heritage, which, being interpreted for our times means: now and in every moment our every past is accepted, our future is opened, our every present is offered to us afresh. This is the truth that sets us free.

✦ ✦ ✦

It's so hard to believe
That it must be said over and over:
"You're O.K., I'm O.K."
God accepts and loves us just as we are.

✦ ✦ ✦

The future is open.
Arise, pick up your life and walk!

✦ ✦ ✦

One fact remains unchanging—God has loved you, is loving you, and will always love you. That's the good news that brings us new life.

✦ ✦ ✦

LEADER: Listen! Here is good news: Jesus said, "I will never turn away anyone who comes to me" (John 6:37b TEV). He has come to forgive you in your failure.

WOMEN: *To accept you as you are,*

MEN: *To set you free,*

ALL: *And to make you what you were meant to be.*

✦ ✦ ✦

Yeah, Jesus—that's the way it is, all right. We can't deny it. We are every name we've called ourselves and some we are afraid to call ourselves. And yet we know that because of your love all our failure is accepted and we are free to live. Hallelujah!

✦ ✦ ✦

God is never far from any of us (Psalm 125:2). We rejoice in this truth that takes the edge of strangeness off life. No matter where we are or what we do, God is with us, still loving us. That's the most fantastic fact of the universe.

✦ ✦ ✦

LEADER: Jesus said, "Neither do I condemn you; go and do not sin again" (John 8:11b). Our life is given back to us with hope.

CONGREGATION: *Every day is an opportunity to decide again that this day shall not be like the others.*

LEADER: That a new person is being created at this moment, free from the past, with the future open.

CONGREGATION: *We have been freed to live fully in the present; that's the good news of the gospel.*

AFFIRMATIONS OF FAITH

We believe that God was in love with the world and could not keep the secret.

The telling of it was CREATION.

We believe that God's love is constantly being shown as creation continues and continues and continues every moment of every day.

We believe that Jesus is our window to divinity and our mirror of humanity. Through Jesus we find God's love for us fully revealed and we discover that God's will for us is that we love one another in full humanness.

We find God's presence of love with us in the Holy Spirit which often speaks to us in the voices of other people. Therefore we affirm that openness to God and openness to other humans are two sides of the same coin and that really listening to others can help us hear God.

We believe that God never gives up on us and that nothing can separate us from God's love.

Alleluia. Amen.

LEADER: Let us affirm together why we worship, for in saying this we will also be affirming our faith.

CONGREGATION: *We worship to reveal ourselves to God and to each other, to look for what we have lost, to glue together broken pieces of life, to refit the scattered jigsaw puzzles of our lives and the world's life, to renew our vision of the life of Jesus Christ, that we might know more sharply and unmistakably what Christ's way really means, to seek to get the point of the greatest drama on earth, to find our own roles and learn our own lines from the director of all history.*

✦ ✦ ✦

I believe in the living God,
    the Parent of all humankind,
    who creates and sustains the universe
    in power and in love.
I believe in Jesus Christ,
    God incarnate on Earth,
    who showed us by his
    words and work,
    suffering with others,
    conquest of death,
    what human life ought to be
    and what God is like.
I believe that the Spirit of God
    is present with us now and always,
    and can be experienced
    in prayer, in forgiveness
    in the Word, the Sacraments,
    the community of the Church
    and in all that we do. Amen.

✦ ✦ ✦

We believe that God never gives up on us.
We believe that Jesus was God in human form
    who showed us the astounding steadfastness
    of God's love for us.
We believe God's Holy Spirit
    is always with us
    even in times of deep suffering and sorrow.
We know that God's love for us
    continues
            and continues
                and continues.

Nothing,
   not even death,
            can separate us from this love.
                             Alleluia!

We believe in the One who gives us life as Creator, and affirm that we are called to be witnesses to this creator God in the world. Therefore, there is no choice for us but to immerse ourselves in the stream of history, accepting our particular place in time and doing the best we can with what we have. We believe that failure to accept responsibility, refusal to take a stand on vital issues, timid rejection of the ties of true belonging are denials of life and of God's will for our lives—they are in fact deeds of death.

We know that the God of all life calls us to affirm life, not die out on it in timidity and fear. God calls us to do our best to understand the times in which we live, to add our weight to the scales on the side of justice and equality within valid differences. We know that if we live our lives responsibly that we need not worry about physical death. Our job is to live out God's love as we have learned it from Jesus right here, right now. God will take care of the rest. *So be it!*

LEADER: Let us recall our faith as God's people.

CONGREGATION: *We believe that God—Creator, Redeemer, and Life Giver—summons the Church to mission in the world:*
    —To witness by word and deed to God's revelation in Christ and the acts of love by which God reconciles us.
    —To evoke in us the personal response of repentance and faith through which we can find newness of life in loving

relationships with God and with our brothers and sisters everywhere.

—To bring us together into a Christian community of worship and love, and to send us forth into the world as servants in the struggle for meaning and justice.

—To move us to live in awareness of the life-giving power of God's presence, in acknowledgement of God's rule over history and in the confident expectation of the final completion of God's purpose. Amen.

LEADER: We are the people of God.

CONGREGATION: *Our lives are eternally significant.*

LEADER: We are the people of the resurrection.

CONGREGATION: *We are free to live to life, and not to death.*

LEADER: We are the people of the covenant.

CONGREGATION: We live our lives in commitment.

LEADER: We are a people of *koinonia.*

CONGREGATION: *We live in mutual love and support.*

LEADER: We are the sons and daughters of God.

CONGREGATION: *We live as a family with all boys and girls, men and women everywhere.*

I believe in the love of God revealed in Jesus Christ.
I believe that behind the clouds of life shines the love of God.
I believe that God has a purpose for the world and a purpose for me.
I believe that God wills the blessedness of all lives and of every single life.

I believe that Jesus Christ saves life from the power of sin and
sorrow and death.

I believe in the life-giving power and grace of the Holy
Spirit.

I believe that through faith and prayer and sacrament I can live
the life which is life indeed.

I believe that God calls me to love and service.

I believe that through Christ life leads at last to the fullness of
goodness, truth, and beauty.

I believe in the grace of Jesus Christ and the love of God and
the communion of the Holy Spirit.

We believe that God still is creating and that we are called to
join in this creation.

We believe that God does not love us because Christ died for
us, but that Christ died for us because God loved us. And
Christ continues to die for us today.

We believe that God's Holy Spirit of love still sets undeserving
people free and that God calls us to help in this task of
liberation.

We believe that "the Church" is a chosen people, not chosen for
its own sake, but to be servants of God for the sake of the
world.

We believe that God's love is something that will never give up
on us, and so we approach the future with confidence.

THE OFFERING

Offertory Prayers
Acts of Dedication

Offertory Prayers

O Giver of Life, behind this offering lies the busy world of our working: the office, the production line, the home, the classroom, the laboratory. Save us from creating a world where wealth accumulates and people decay. Accept this offering and our lives, limited as they may be, as willing instruments for good in your world. Amen.

✦ ✦ ✦

We bring you what we have, God: our good intentions, our mixed motives, our limited grasp of truth, our halfhearted commitment, our tiny gifts. None of it, we know, is good enough, but we offer them anyway. And we dare to affirm that it is received. In Jesus' name, Amen.

✦ ✦ ✦

Mother God, who loves us, in this act we present ourselves: our work and our leisure, our joys and our sorrows, our thoughts and our deeds—just as we are, to be used by you in the world. We humbly ask you to accept our offering as the personal giving of ourselves for the increase of good and in the service of truth, here, and all over the earth. Amen.

✦ ✦ ✦

God, as we offer our money to you, help us also to be able to offer you ourselves. Take our bodies, our minds, and our spirits and use them for your ministry in your world. Through Jesus Christ, Amen.

✦ ✦ ✦

God, we know that your gifts cannot be hoarded, that they are for spending. Help us in this time of offering to share with you not only our money but our lives also. How do we need to spend ourselves today? Amen.

✦ ✦ ✦

God, before the gifts you have given us, our gifts pale into insignificance. We are almost ashamed to bring these gifts, because they cost us so little. And yet we know that just as you accept us though we be unworthy you accept our gifts. Increase our vision and enlarge our compassion, that we might embrace all the world's needs as those which demand a response from us, so that in this world there *shall* be celebration. Amen.

✦ ✦ ✦

Clothe the naked and you clothe Jesus—that's what you said, God. Help us to hear those words—really hear them so that we can begin to discover that the distance to Heaven is measured by nakedness, hunger, thirst. Help us to hear these words so well that we begin to give accordingly. Amen.

✦ ✦ ✦

Mother/Father, help us to realize that silver and gold are not God, whether in the form of a golden calf or a bargain counter. Help us to give ourselves fully to you today as we share our money in this offering. In Jesus' name we pray, Amen.

✦ ✦ ✦

God, we know that "offering" means giving all that we have and are. Help us to do just that today. *So be it.*

Acts of Dedication

LEADER: Our message is that God was reconciling all persons through Christ, not counting their trespasses against them.

CONGREGATION: *And entrusting to us the message of reconciliation. So we are ambassadors for Christ; God appealing to needy humanity through us* (II Corinthians 5:19, 20 adapted). *In a broken world where we have nothing to lose but everything, we accept with humility and awe this invitation to be agents of Christ's reconciling love in the world.*

LEADER: The God of all history needs and calls us to be agents of love. We are sent into the world to be concerned and caring people.

CONGREGATION: *Send us, God. Send us next door, into the next room, to speak somehow to a human heart beating alongside ours. Send us to be bearers of dignity in a sub-human, hopeless situation. Send us to show joy in a moment and a place where there has been no joy but only the will to die.*

Send us to reflect your light in the darkness of futility, hopelessness, and the horror of human cruelty. But give us your light, too, God, in our own darkness and need. Amen.

LEADER: There is so much to be done. "Dedication" means deciding to be the one to do it.

CONGREGATION: *Because God loves us, we can know what it is to love others. Let us go forth boldly into the world, obedi-*

ently, decisively, lovingly, joyfully, to bring God's peace and life to all.

✦ ✦ ✦

LEADER: Christ Jesus, whose death and resurrection we remember, and whose second coming we await:

CONGREGATION: *With your help we will do our best*
To say the word,
And do the work,
And be the person
In whom our neighbors may see
God's reign coming near
And God's holy love revealed.

LEADER: Servants of Christ, the Savior Jesus accepts our honest intentions, and will give us the help we need to perform them faithfully.

CONGREGATION: *God help us so to do.*

✦ ✦ ✦

LEADER: Who are you?

   Left: We are the people who once were lost but now have been found.

   Right: We have been found for a purpose. We have been given a job.

CONGREGATION: *It is for us to love as we have been loved, to die as others have died for us.*

LEADER: Then go forth to your task in the knowledge of your acceptance before God; be present to life as it is given to you; and remember your obligation to every creation; in the name of God the Creator, Redeemer and Sustainer. God be with you.

CONGREGATION: *And with your spirit.*

LEADER: Amen.

CONGREGATION: *Amen.*

BENEDICTIONS

LEADER: Go now, remembering what we have done here. Go, remembering that you are a forgiven people, eternally loved, thoughtfully instructed, gratefully obedient, responding, and responsible wherever you are. You can never be the same again.

CONGREGATION: *We know. We go to be God's people in the world.*

LEADER: May God's peace and joy go with you. So be it.

CONGREGATION: *So be it!*

✦ ✦ ✦

LEADER: Go forth now into a world where apathy and half-heartedness are dominant. Move the world a little. In the name of God the Creator, Redeemer, and Sustainer. God be with you.

CONGREGATION: *And with you.*

LEADER: Amen.

CONGREGATION: *Amen.*

✦ ✦ ✦

LEADER: With your love deep in our hearts,

CONGREGATION: *God go with us;*

LEADER: With your wisdom to know and understand,

CONGREGATION: *God go with us;*

LEADER: With your Spirit stirring in our souls,

CONGREGATION: *God go with us;*

LEADER: With your power to care and share in your world,

CONGREGATION: *God go with us to a new day. Amen.*

✦ ✦ ✦

LEADER: May God's grace, mercy, and strength be with you.

CONGREGATION: *And may we be instruments of God's grace, mercy, and strength to the world in which we live. Amen.*

✦ ✦ ✦

Go now in the confident knowledge that God gives you strength, hope, love, and peace. Alleluia!

✦ ✦ ✦

Now may you go with God into the sunlight of new relationship in which you can be a light for people who are desperately searching for love and care. Amen.

✦ ✦ ✦

Today is the first day of the rest of your life and
The last day of the first of your life.
Live it as both a beginning and an end,
With the hope that new beginnings bring,
With the commitment that endings demand,
Knowing in all you do that God's love is with you,
Sustaining, supporting, encouraging. Amen.

✤7✤

Liberated Services

THE SERVICES that follow are complete in that they give specific suggestions for every part of a service developed around a specific theme. However, they are included here only as examples of what can be done in liberating the liturgy. They are for your use, and that means you should feel free to adapt them to your own particular situation and your own special liturgical style.

We have tried to list a variety of available hymns—both traditional and contemporary. All of the traditional hymns are found in *The Book of Hymns* of the United Methodist Church and in other traditional hymn books. We have listed one source for each folk hymn listed, although often they may be found in many different books. In some cases, we have rewritten former sexist hymns or added new words to an old tune, and here we have included the new words for your use.

Part of liberating the liturgy, as we have said, is to see new possibilities for our old forms. This is true in every section of the liturgy, but perhaps especially in the sermon. Thus, we have included suggestions for very nontraditional sermons. If these seem unusable in your particular situation, certainly the same ideas can be incorporated into a more traditional sermon. We hope, however, you'll seriously consider the possibility of trying something new with the sermon and with other parts of the liturgy. Our suggestions here are only a feeble beginning for what you and your friends can do if you let your imaginations loose. We hope you'll do just that.

FINDING ACCEPTANCE AND SELF-WORTH FROM GOD

Prelude

Songs emphasizing our need for acceptance and self-worth such as "I Am, . . ." "I Gotta Be Me," et cetera.

Call to Worship

LEADER: We come to this service with so many needs and longings. We've been many different places, conceived many different thoughts.

CONGREGATION: *But underneath all our differences is the same basic need for love and acceptance.*

LEADER: And that's why we're here—to admit to each other our need for love,

CONGREGATION: *And to celebrate the most marvelous fact of the universe—that God loves us and accepts us just as we are. Alleluia!*

Hymn

"Love Divine, All Loves Excelling"; or "Saints and Sinners" from *Songbook for Saints and Sinners*, edited by Carlton R. Young; or "Day by Day" from *The Genesis Songbook*, edited by Carlton R. Young.

Invocation

God, you are both heavenly Father and Mother to us and we know you are with us at all times. But we pause to ask early in this service that your Spirit of love especially surround and invade us as we worship here today. We really want to know you, God. Be with us now. Amen.

Call to Confession

To be open to God we must be honest with ourselves no matter how painful or distasteful this may be. We have missed the mark of our high calling. Let us confess this to God.

General Prayer of Confession
(Prayed by all)

Sometimes we feel hopeless and afraid, God. Does anyone really care about us? Do our lives really make any difference when we look at the whole universe—when we see so many other people who are more talented, rich, and famous than we? Sometimes too, the fact of our own impending death sinks into us, and we're scared. Is there eternal life? If there is, what's it like? Why can't we trust you that everything will be O.K. no matter what? And yet all the nagging doubts about death and life are still there. Forgive us for our doubts and fears, God. We know that often they make us treat others cruelly. Forgive us for all the evil we've done to others in the name of our own anxieties. In Jesus' name, Amen.

Words of Assurance

LEADER: A sparrow falters.

CONGREGATION: *Life goes on.*

LEADER: A sparrow falls.

CONGREGATION: *Creation's castoffs.*

LEADER: Yet forever received and affirmed.

CONGREGATION: *Even the sparrow finds a home.*

LEADER: You are accepted.

CONGREGATION: *Accepted by that which is greater than ourselves.*

LEADER: Do not ask for the name now.

CONGREGATION: *Do not try to do anything now.*

LEADER: Do not seek for anything, perform anything, intend anything.

CONGREGATION: *Simply accept the fact that we are accepted.*

LEADER: Forever received and affirmed.

CONGREGATION: *Even the sparrow finds a home.*

Scripture Readings

Old Testament: A paraphrase of Psalm 8.

O God, our God,
Your greatness is seen in all the world!
Your glory reaches to the heavens,
  Even children and babies sing your praise.
You have built a fortress because of your foes,
  to still the enemy and the revengeful.

When I look at the sky, the work of your fingers,
    at the moon and the stars, which you have made—
What are we, that you think of us;
And our children, that you should care for them?

Yet you made us but a little less than you yourself;
And you crowned us with glory and honor!

You made us rulers over all you have made;
You gave us responsibility for all things:
   sheep and cattle, and wild animals too;
   the birds and the fish,
   and all the creatures in the seas.
God, our God,
   your greatness is seen in all the world.

New Testament: Matthew 25:14–30

Affirmation of Faith

We believe in the infinite worth of every human being. We believe that our worth is ultimately derived not by what others think of us or even by what we think of ourselves, but by what God thinks of us. We affirm that God loves each of us with a richness and depth that is beyond our wildest imaginings.

We believe that every human being falters and fails at times and needs the forgiving love of God to keep going. We know that each of us becomes deadened to our world and our brothers and sisters, and so we need the enlivening power of God's Holy Spirit to be with us bringing us alive inside.

Each of us faces the terrifying unknown we call death. And that is why God's promise of eternal life sealed in Jesus holds out so much hope to us. We know that even though our lives may be filled with great trouble and sorrow that God never deserts us, never gives up on us. With this faith firm in our hearts we can shout with the saints of all the ages. Alleluia!

New Ways of Doing a Sermon

1. You may want to have three persons from your community who have struggled with the questions of acceptance and self-worth share with the community what has happened to them

on their journey through life. If there is time, you might then want to divide the congregation into small groups so they can react to what was said and share some of their own personal struggles.

2. You might like to divide your congregation into small groups and let them sculpture from junk materials (clay, paper, rubber bands, balloons, paper clips, toothpicks, scraps of cloth, whatever you have available) their response as a small group to the words of assurance or the affirmation of faith. They could then bring their finished creations forward as part of the offering, and, if you have time, you might want a spokesperson from each group to share with everyone some of the group's thinking as they made what they did.

3. You might want to ask a small group from your congregation to work ahead of time on acting out a contemporary version of the New Testament lesson. This could then be presented as the sermon along with comments from the congregation and/or the minister.

4. If you have some persons in your group who are skilled dancers, you may want to ask them to do a dance based on the paraphrase of Psalm 8. This too could be an effective part of a sermon. Remember, if you pick the last two alternatives, try to ask the people who are going to work on them in plenty of time so that there will not be undue pressure on them. Even several months early is not too soon.

Hymn

"O Thou Who Art the Shepherd" (You will want to change the word "Father" in verse two to "God"), "Love Them Now," from *The Genesis Songbook*, or "Magic Penny," from *New Wine: Songs for Celebration*, edited by Jim Strathdee and Nelson Stringer.

Offertory Prayer

God, money is important. Sometimes we get to thinking that it's the most important thing in the world. We know that's not true, God, and that thinking like that can destroy us if we're not careful. Help us now to make an honest gift of our money and of ourselves in the service of your love. Amen.

[The time of the offering is also ideal to have a sharing of joys and concerns from the community. The apostle Paul says that the church should be the kind of community where we weep with those who weep and rejoice with those who rejoice. But in order to do this we need to know the special things that may be in peoples' hearts. In a small congregation this sharing can be spontaneous. Led by the minister or a lay person, the congregation is simply invited to share some of their special joys and concerns from the past week. This can be a beautiful community-building experience. After concerns and joys have been shared, a time of silence can be observed when these concerns and joys along with others which were not expressed are brought before God in prayer. Or the minister or a lay person can pray aloud a spontaneous prayer which incorporates these joys and concerns of the community. If the congregation is large, it may be necessary to ask certain persons to serve as representatives of the total congregation to come before the whole group and share particular joys and concerns they have had this week or that they know others have experienced during the week. Different persons should do this each week and all those who do it should be encouraged to keep their presentations brief. The purpose is not to preach a sermon or give a long history, but simply to state a joy or concern that has been experienced by someone in the congregation.

Another way to do the offering is to have the congregation

process around the church to place their money offering in strategically located baskets while singing an offertory song such as the one at the end of this suggested service. Such physical movement is often good. It impresses upon everyone that the offering is not just dropping some money in a plate as it comes by, but that it involves the presenting of your whole body to God.]

Act of Dedication

LEADER: "People who need people are the luckiest people in the world."

CONGREGATION: *We need people and people need us.*

LEADER: To be a Christian is to be alive to these needs in ourselves and others and respond to them.

CONGREGATION: *Well, let's get busy!*

Hymn

"Take My Life and Let It Be Consecrated" or "All That I Am," from *Songbook for Saints and Sinners.*

Benediction

[Instead of a spoken benediction, let each person turn to his or her neighbor and affirm that person with a handshake and one word that means acceptance to himself/herself.]

CELEBRATING GOD

For Your Meditation

How do you image-ine God? Could it be that God's aliveness is
not static, but moving? Could God also be in process, continually becoming? How could God be anything else if God loves us?
Love implies process, the capacity to change with the needs of
the person who is loved. To image-ine God then, we need moving images—kinetic sculpture, film, multiple images and colors.
As Buckminster Fuller says, "For God, to me, it seems is a verb,
not a noun."

Call to Worship

LEADER: Welcome to an adventure that can be the most excit-
ing adventure of your life.

CONGREGATION: *But we came to a worship service.*

LEADER: Worship is an adventure, for in worship we attempt
to be in communion with One of whom we can know something, but whom we cannot wholly know.

CONGREGATION: *Even while we experience God's presence we
know that there are other dimensions of God we have not
yet experienced.*

LEADER: God is like the horizon. We see the horizon, we experience it, but when we get there it's always out beyond us.

CONGREGATION: *So let us give ourselves totally today to worshipping the beyond in our midst.*

Hymn

"Immortal, Invisible, God Only Wise" (substitute "Mother" for "Father" when it is used for the second time in verse 4); "Clap Your Hands," from *Hymnal for Young Christians* and many other songbooks.

(Note suggested changes in this hymn on p. 30 of Chapter 4. Also, in verse 4, "brotherhood" should be changed to "unity." "So with your fellow man let's all join hand to hand" should be changed to "So with our friends we stand united hand in hand." In verse 5, "man" should be changed to "one" and "our fellowmen" should be changed to "every human.")

Invocation

God, we pray that your spirit may fill our spirits today so that we come alive in new ways to your reality. Amen.

Call to Confession

[Read some newspaper headlines and follow with this statement.]

The world is in agony and although we know we are by no means responsible for all the world's sorrow, we also know that we have added to it by what we have done and failed to do. Let us confess our sins before God.

General Prayer of Confession

God, we come before you today aching inside. We are revolted by the news that comes to us daily of hatred and war. But we are doubly troubled today because we know that the awful things we see going on in the world are also inside of us to one

degree or another. We know, too, God, that often we have tried
to go our lives alone without calling on your help. We haven't
even been willing to take the time to see how an expanded
concept of you might bring us to a brand new way of envision-
ing possibilities for ourselves. We need to experience today the
radical, sweeping power of your active love in the midst of our
halting and hesitant living. Amen.

Words of Assurance

Look around you—God's powerful love is present in persons
who care about you and about social justice for the world.

Look within you—God's powerful love is present in all your
yearnings to be the very best person you possibly can be.

Hymn

"God????" (Tune: "Lonesome Valley")

We have come to ask some questions
We have to ask them by ourselves.
Oh, nobody else can ask them for us.
We have to ask them for ourselves.

How can we begin to find God
When God is so beyond our grasp?
Oh, when will we know God fully present?
This is the question we must ask.

Now we see with cloudy vision
What we'll know when we shall die.
Yet we can see now fantastic glimpses
Of God's strong love for which we cry.

So let us keep our questions coming
Let us be bold to ask them clear.

For searching we find tremendous insight
Into God's love that's present here.

Scripture Readings

Old Testament: Isaiah 42:10–17
New Testament: Luke 15:8–10
(Note that the first passage compares God to both a man and a
woman. The second pictures God as a woman and is part of a
trilogy of analogies which portrays God as both a man and a
woman.)

New Ways of Doing a Sermon

[You might want to send out a group from your church, a few
weeks before this service, with cassette recorders to interview
persons on the street with the question, "What do you think
God is like?" A committee could then edit these comments
down to about five minutes of the most interesting and this
could be used to kick off discussion about who God is. Youth
groups might be especially excited by such a project. After the
tape presentation perhaps the minister and someone of the
opposite sex could do a dialogue reflecting on the nature of God.
Such a dialogue might be open-ended with time for questions
and comments from the congregation. You might also want to
divide your congregation into several small discussion groups
which could tackle various questions about God such as the
following: Is it proper to think of God anthropomorphically as
either male or female? (Note that the scripture passages men-
tioned above see God as female.) What does it mean to say God
is a verb? Is it valuable to concieve of God as an active force
rather than as a person? Do you like this way of thinking? Are
there ways of preserving the meaning of the concept of God as
Father without being sexist? What are they? After the groups

have batted these questions around a bit, they could then come together and share some of their insights with the total group. The minister or someone else would want to help direct this sharing and perhaps add some comments of his or her own.

It would also be possible to begin the whole service by passing out a short questionnaire on which provocative statements about God were placed along with blanks for persons to check if they agree, disagree, or are neutral with each statement. The sermon could then be a group discussion of these statements or, if this does not seem feasible, the minister could develop his or her sermon around what the statements on the questionnaire told him or her about God.

Another alternative would be to ask some of the members of your younger children's church school classes to draw a picture of God. You could then make slides of these pictures and show them at the beginning of the sermon to give persons a child's-eye view of God. Discussion, dialogue, or a straight monologue sermon could then flow from these pictures.]

Offertory Prayer

God, we know that all we have comes from you, but these gifts are made for spending, not for hoarding. So now as we share some of our material wealth, help us also to share all our talents as agents of your love in the world. Amen.

[The same suggestions made in the offering section of the service "Finding Acceptance and Self-Worth from God" would be appropriate here.]

Hymn

(To the tune of "Michael Row the Boat Ashore")

> God is love and God is light
> Hal-le-lu-jah!

God can help us gain new sight
Hal-le-lu-jah!

We must hear God's call to us.
Hal-le-lu-jah!
To love everyone's a must
Hal-le-lu-jah!

God is here yet far away
Hal-le-lu-jah!
But God hears the needs we pray
Hal-le-lu-jah!

God is neither up nor down
Hal-le-lu-jah!
But God's everywhere around
Hal-le-lu-jah!

God's in me and God's in you
Hal-le-lu-jah!
So all folk are sacred, too
Hal-le-lu-jah!

Benediction

(Adapted from an ancient Navajo benediction)

God is before us.
God is behind us.
God is above us.
God is below us.
God's words shall come from our mouths
For we are God's essence, a sign of God's love
All is finished in beauty
All is finished in beauty
All is finished in beauty
All is finished in beauty.

CELEBRATING LIBERATION FROM ROLE STEREOTYPES

A Service of Holy Communion

Call to Worship

LEADER: Christ's love is a liberating love.

CONGREGATION: *It sets us free to be the beautiful people we can be.*

LEADER: In worship we come together to celebrate and call upon Christ's liberating power for our lives.

CONGREGATION: *To be free is to be our own person and to know that the basic power of the universe which we call God is all for us in our struggle to be our best.*

Hymn

"In Christ There Is No East or West" (Change the last line of verse 2 to read "That binds all hu-man-kind.")

(Verse 3 should be changed to the following:

Join hands, then, friends of the faith,
What-e-'er your race may be.
Who serves the God of life and love
Is sure-ly kin to me.)

Alternate hymn: "They'll Know We Are Christians By Our Love." (Change "man's" in verse 3 to "one's.")

(Verse 4 should be as follows:

All praise to our Maker
From whom all things come.

All praise to Christ Jesus
Who the victory won.
All praise to the Spirit
Who makes us one.)

Invocation

God, lay the freeing power of your Spirit on us in this service
so that we are made restless to strive for liberation from old role
stereotypes and old sins. Amen.

Call to Confession

We can only be free to be new people when we face the past
honestly and admit our wrongs. Let's do that now.

General Prayer of Confession

MEN: We confess that too often we have caged you women into
   rigid categories and have seen you either as temptress or
   virgin mother. We have not allowed you to be unique and
   beautiful individuals.

WOMEN: We confess that we have sometimes encouraged you
   to stereotype us by manipulating you with our sexuality or
   by deifying our role as mother.

MEN: We confess that we have been too willing to let you
   women be our servants doing the menial tasks that we
   considered beneath us. We know now that such lording it
   over you often made us unable to answer Christ's call to be
   servants of all humanity without regard to status or position.

WOMEN: We confess that we have for too long let you men
   assume roles of dominance even when it causes you to be

miserable and die young from heart attacks. We know now that always doing menial tasks is not what Christ means when he calls us to servanthood. We should not refuse menial tasks, but we should not refuse tasks that contain great responsibility either.

MEN: We have made a god out of sports because our daily jobs are based on competition.

WOMEN: We have contented ourselves with bazaars, fashion shows, and soap operas because our tasks were too boring.

MEN: We have spent our lives using the wrong set of priorities. People hunger for Christ's love while we watch pro-football.

WOMEN: We have spent our lives using the wrong set of priorities. People hunger for Christ's love while we watch soap operas.

MEN: Our greatest sin has been too much pride. We have wanted to control the world.

WOMEN: Our greatest sin has been too little pride. We have yielded up control to others.

MEN: We have heard your confession, and we assure you that God has also heard. As God promised forgiveness for all the sins of all people, we share that forgiveness with you by forgiving you in the name of God the Creator, Jesus the Redeemer, and the Holy Spirit, the Sustainer of all life.

WOMEN: We have heard your confession, and we assure you that God has also heard. As God promised forgiveness for all the sins of all people, we share that forgiveness with you by forgiving you in the name of God the Creator, Jesus the Redeemer, and the Holy Spirit, the Sustainer of life.

Doxology

"Praise God, from Whom All Blessings Flow"
   (Either use the traditional "Old 100th" hymn tune or a new tune such as the one done by Avery and Marsh in *Songbook for Saints and Sinners.* The words should be as follows:

> Praise God, from whom all blessings flow;
> Praise God, all creatures here be-low;
> Praise God a-bove, ye heaven-ly host;
> Praise Ma-ker, Christ, and Ho-ly Ghost. Amen.)

Scripture Readings

Old Testament: Genesis 1:26–31
New Testament: Galatians 3:23–28

New Ways of Doing A Sermon

[The sermon could take many forms. It could be a straight exposition on the Scripture passages drawing from them God's concern that each of us be full human beings seen beyond any particular roles imposed upon us by society or ourselves. The sermon could also be a dialogue between a man and a woman in which they shared what the Scripture passages meant to them and how they have begun to achieve liberation from role stereotypes. Part of the sermon could be an impromptu drama showing some of the tragic humor of our role stereotyping. Some excellent plays and articles have been written which help us to see how ridiculous some of our roles are today. Naturally, if a play is done, you'll have to do advance preparation with your actors and actresses. It need not be a production of professional quality, however, but simply good enough to get its point across with humor and clarity. You might also want to show the film "Anything You Want to Be."* This short film shows how much a young girl's vocational aspirations are influenced and shaped by the roles women are expected to play. After the film, comments could be made relating it to the whole question of role enslavement and the Christian call to liberation. Also small group discussion could be a part of reaction to this film or to any of the other means suggested for doing the sermon.]

Hymn

"Bread of the World" or "Take Our Bread," by Joe Wise, in *Songbook for Saints and Sinners* and many other folk hymnals. (Change "Father" to "God.")

[As this hymn is being sung representatives of the congregation should bring the Communion elements forward and place them on the worship table.]

[After the hymn the minister will lift the bread and wine.]

MINISTER: The gifts of God for the people of God.
[The minister will then lift the loaf of bread as he or she breaks it.]

MINISTER: Christ's body was broken so that we might be whole.
[The minister will then lift the wine.]

MINISTER: Christ's blood was shed so that we might be transfused with God's love.

[Try to make the way you serve Communion demonstrate what you are trying to communicate about the liberating power of God's love. If we really mean that this love breaks down role stereotypes, then we should be willing to let all Christians serve

*Available from the Audio-Visual Education Center, University of Michigan, 416 Fourth Street, Ann Arbor, Michigan.

one another in Communion. This is essentially what already happens in churches where Communion is taken in the pews. But even if it is taken by coming forward, still the "priesthood of all believers" should allow us to serve one another. If there is room, you might want to ask persons to come forward in small groups and stand together in a circle, each serving his or her neighbor the elements. By having small groups come forward and sit together at a table, you could achieve the same purpose. You may want to have special music during the receiving of Communion. You may want to have persons receive it in silence. You may want to have them say their own words of love and care to one another as they serve each other. Each congregation and each physical setting is different so it will be up to you to come up with the most effective way of sharing Communion together. You may want to encourage people to bring their offering as they come forward to take Communion, or you may want to have the offering at another time.]

Prayer of Thanksgiving
(Prayed by all)

God, our human history is a record of your love for us. Many years ago our ancestors in the faith were called by you to celebrate the Passover to remember how you rescued your people from slavery. Today we have celebrated a new Passover and a new covenant as in this Communion we remember Christ's loving death for us all. We know this death, too, is a freeing from slavery, not just of a political nature but of all kinds. In this service we are especially grateful to you for calling us to a responsible freedom which goes beyond all kinds of role stereotypes. In Christ's name we pray, Amen.

Hymn

(To tunes No. 5 and No. 294, "I Love Thy Kingdom, Lord," in
The Book of Hymns (United Methodist), words by Martha Montague Wilson.

> Yes, all are one in Christ, Whose one baptism share;
> Not Jew or Gentile, slave or free, Not male or female be.

> In Christ all barriers fall, One people—all are we;
> The children of bright promises, Christ comes to make us
> free.

> The gift of life we share, The chains of slavery fall;
> And women, men, from every land, Give answer to Christ's
> call.

> So stand in Christ and live, The life of faith and love;
> Sing: All are one in Christ, Who leads to joy here and above.

Benediction

The Passing of the Peace.

[Have each person greet his or her neighbor with a handshake
and an embrace and these words: "The peace of God go with
you my sister (brother)." The response: "And with you my
brother (sister)."]

A WEDDING SERVICE

Before we present a sample contemporary wedding service, a few preliminary comments are in order. A whole book could be done, and we understand some are in the making, which would deal with the wedding service. This is not the place for such a book, but a few comments are essential. First it is important to realize that the Church only got into the wedding ceremony fairly recently. Marriage was a wholly civil ceremony until about the tenth century. Thus many of the customs which we still find in today's ceremonies are totally pagan and come down to us from a time when women were considered the property of men. The "giving away of the bride" by her father, for example, is a throwback to the old custom when the bride was sold to the prospective groom. Some attempts have been made to redeem this part of the traditional wedding ceremony by reinterpreting it to mean that this giving away of the bride is symbolic of the blessing the parents of the families bestow upon the new couple. If this is an appropriate interpretation, however, why isn't the symbolism more in line with it? You'll note that in our service the parental blessing is obvious and the giving away of the bride is eliminated.

More and more ministers are encouraging couples to write their own services. We see this as a healthy sign when it is done with real care and with the help of someone skilled in liturgy, such as the minister.* It is important for couples who are attempting to write their own service to realize that they do not have to come up with an all new service. Sections from other contemporary services may speak to them and they will want to use them. Also parts of the traditional service may still be

*For much more detailed help in designing wedding ceremonies see our cassette resource entitled "It's Your Wedding," Creative Resources, A Division of Word Inc., April, 1971.

what they want to use. The vows of many traditional services have a power and poetry that makes them effective even in a service that is largely contemporary.

We believe that a wedding service is especially for the couple to be married and that their tastes should govern how the service is developed. We should not attempt to impose our musical or poetic tastes upon them. We do have a responsibility to help them have a theologically and socially responsible service, however. It is hoped that persons can use the service that follows as a guide which can give them ideas as they develop their own wedding service.

THE SERVICE OF WORSHIP

CELEBRATING THE MARRIAGE

OF

_____(name of bride)_____

and

_____(name of groom)_____

_____(the date)_____

Prelude

[Whatever musical style is especially meaningful to the couple should be used during the service.]

Call to Worship

MINISTER: On this special day we gather for this special service to celebrate the wedding of two special people.

CONGREGATION: *This is a day for singing and rejoicing, for balloons and butterflies.*

MINISTER: Alleluia, praise to God.

CONGREGATION: *Alleluia, praise to God!*

Processional

[Both bride and groom come in gaily together, along with their especially close friends and relatives. As they come in everyone sings the hymn.]

Hymn

"This Is the Day," from *Hymns for Now II*, edited by Steyer and Firnhaber.
(Add this verse between verses 3 and 4:

This is the day when we share our love.
Let us be glad and re-joice in it!
This is the day when we share our love.)

Invocation

Gracious God, may your spirit inform and inspire this service of worship, and may it always guide the two who are to be joined in marriage today and all of us here who witness this event. Amen.

Call to Confession

Even at times of exquisite happiness like this we must be reminded that we know better than we do. Let us confess our sins before God.

General Prayer of Confession

God, this is a service celebrating love and so we are reminded
of how often we have failed to be loving; celebrating the creation of a new family, and we remember how often we have
taken our own families for granted and failed to see possibilities
for fulfillment in them. Two people today are pledging themselves to be "all for" each other, and yet our lives are strewn
with pledges seriously made and then lightly broken. We have
not loved as we should; we have not been with and for our
families as we could, and too often we have been untrue to our
commitments. May our participation in the creation of this new
relationship help us to reexamine and then renew all our relationships through Jesus Christ our Lord. Amen.

Words of Assurance

The God who created us can re-create us. This is the truth that
sets us free.

Scripture Readings

The Old Testament: Psalm 150
The New Testament: I Corinthians 13

Contemporary Reading

[A passage from some contemporary writing that has been
especially meaningful to the couple is read.]

Sermon Meditation

[Here the minister who is performing the ceremony could be
invited to share some of his or her insights about the meaning

of marriage or of a particular word or phrase in the marriage
covenant. This might also be a time when the couple themselves would want to share with the group assembled some of
their understandings about marriage and life in general.]

The Covenant of Marriage

[Where blanks are given for the names of the bride and groom,
it is appropriate to alternate the order in which they appear.]

Opening Remarks

This is it, a moment packed with anticipation, when standing
before God and this group of friends and relatives _____
_____ and _____ pledge them-
selves to one another in the covenant of marriage.

We hope that those of you who are married will take this
occasion to renew your own vows, and that all of you will share
in this celebration by offering your own personal prayers for this
couple ready to begin a new life together.

The Charge to the Bride and Groom

To the Christian, marriage is neither a casual nor a socially
legislated business arrangement. It is a holy covenant between
two persons who love each other. _____
and _____, your marriage is one of the most
sacred and most treasured parts of your life. It is a celebration
of all the mystery and wonder that deep love brings to living.
It is also a recognition, however, that love and marriage are not
always easy and that along with the tenderness, newness, and
joy in a marriage, a marriage must overcome many forces that
might destroy it. Love is dynamic and will fly away from a
marriage which has become static and unbending. When love

lives, as it does here today, it reflects the deepest and most
tender secrets of the universe.

And I charge you, _____ and you, _____
_____, with the responsibility to keep alive; to
grow, to change, to maintain the capacity for wonder, for spontaneity, for humor; to remain flexible, warm, and sensitive. Give
fully to each other, show your real feelings to one another, save
time for each other, no matter what demands are made upon
your day. I charge you to nurture each other to fullness and
wholeness, realizing that each of you will need at times to bring
strength and support and worth to the other. I charge you, as
you grow to love each other more deeply, to discover out of this
love a love for all of creation in which the mystery of your love
has happened.

The Questions

[The bride and groom shall each be asked the following questions.]

Do you find within you a special love for _____
_____ that convinces you that you want to spend the rest of
your lives together?

Do you find within you the courage to resist the many deaths
by which love can die?

Are you willing to love _____ into
his/her unique fullness and to take the risk and accept the
vulnerability of love again and again and again? (Each question
is to be answered in the appropriate affirmative.)

The Blessing of the Families

MINISTER: Who give their blessing to this marriage and in the
giving say an enthusiastic "Yes!" to this new relationship?

FAMILIES: *We do. Yes! Amen.*

The Wedding Vows

[With the bride and groom facing each other, each makes his/her offering to the other, feeling free to add personal comments to the vows.]

> I offer my love; I offer my strength; I offer my support; I offer my loyalty; I offer my faith; I offer my hope—in all the changing circumstances of life—as long as we both shall live.

The Giving of the Rings

MINISTER: What symbols do you bring as evidence of the vows you have just taken?

THE COUPLE: *These rings.*

MINISTER: These rings mark the beginning of a life journey together filled with wonder, surprises, laughter, tears, celebration, grief, and joy. May these rings be a sign to you of the continuing love you have pledged to one another today.

[If the congregation attending the wedding is small enough, the couple may wish to pass their wedding rings around to the worshippers. Each person is asked to make a silent prayer for the couple as he/she touches these tokens of their love with her/his fingers. In this way the whole congregation can actively participate in the blessing of the rings.]

[With the bride and groom facing each other, each places the ring on the other's finger and says these words.]

> I give you this sign of my love, knowing that love is precious and fragile, yet strong. Whenever I see your ring I will remember all that I have pledged to you here this day.

The Response of the Congregation

As members of Christ's Church, we rejoice with you in the covenant you have made. We pledge to support and strengthen your life together, to speak the truth to you in love, and with you to seek to live a life of love for others.

A Prayer

O God, we pray that this couple and all who are gathered here will grow in the understanding and experience of love. As _____ and _____ become bound closer to each other, may they also ever be more surely themselves. To your tender and watchful care we here commit _____ and _____. In health and sickness, in abundance and want, in life and death, abide with them that they shall never withdraw from you. Through Jesus Christ. Amen.

The Declaration

You have now publicly shared your love for and special commitment to one another. Explore this love well with deep reverence. Explore it with joy and hope and perseverance. I now pronounce you husband and wife, according to the Spirit and in accord with human law.

Benediction

Today is a new beginning in the lives of _____ _____ and _____. May God's peace and love go with them as they continue life's journey. Amen.

Recessional

"Morning Has Broken." (This song is to be sung by all as the wedding party leaves.)

Postlude

(Something joyful!)

❖8❖

How to Handle Objections
to Changes
in Your Service

PERHAPS THIS CHAPTER should have been entitled "How to Introduce Changes into Your Worship Service in Such a Way that Objections Never Materialize." Certainly the first way to handle objections should be to prevent them from ever occurring. But how do we do that?

What follows are some guidelines that we have found helpful in working with congregations experiencing change in their worship. What we say is necessarily rather general and will need to be adapted or perhaps totally changed by you as you assess your particular situation. For some of you, our ideas may seem old hat or simply common sense. For us, many of them came with arduous and sometimes quite painful experiences. We hope they are helpful to you.

The first rule in all communication, and especially communication concerned with bringing about change within a community, is love and accept the other persons for who they are. No matter how right we are, if we present our arguments from a standpoint of superiority, we are in trouble from the start. All of us have probably known persons who were tremendously intelligent and often had great ideas, but who could never get anyone to agree with them. Their manner of presenting their concepts automatically made people want to argue with them.

They seemed so cocky, so sure, so know-it-all. That's a sure way to get into trouble in communication.

To communicate in love means to listen with your whole being to the other person. It means to attempt to hear what that person is really saying, not just with his or her words but also by the meaning and feeling behind those words.

To communicate in love means to accept the other person even though we may disagree completely with what she/he believes. It means being willing to take time with the other person and build up trusting relationships with that person.

Unless your community of faith is extremely small, it will be impossible for you to do all this communicating in love by yourself. You will need to train others to help you so that persons in your community can have a chance to express themselves personally on this issue. In churches with large memberships you will need to be a resource to the resource persons. But no matter what the size of the situation the basic strategy of communicating in love personally with others in your community must remain.

Even a concern to communicate with others in love and acceptance will not prevail by itself. Coupled with this must be a clear and rational presentation of what sexism is and does. The earlier chapters in this book should help you develop such a rationale.

Someone has said that a group will accept anything if it's explained the right way. That may be a bit of an exaggeration, but it is far more true than most of us realize. To explain something in the right way generally means to use all the channels of communication open to you. This means that in addition to small study groups and one-to-one dialogue on sexism and worship, informative articles about the subject should occasionally appear in your church's newsletter and sermons should sometimes deal specifically with this issue or at least make passing reference to it. Organized groups within the church should be encouraged to tackle the issue and have several discussion groups work on it.

It is important to approach all these channels of communication with great sensitivity, however. It does much more harm than good to have a group deal negatively with the issue. It should only be brought up in a group when you feel a sufficient number of people have their levels of awareness raised to bring about a positive discussion of the issue. Articles in your newsletter and comments in sermons should also be handled with great sensitivity. It is important not to overkill with constant references to the subject. It is also good to vary your approach to the subject so that sometimes you talk of how women feel in sexist services while at other times you point out ways of interpreting many of the sexist passages of the Bible or discuss new concepts of God.

It is also important to recognize that it may be necessary to move gradually in bringing actual changes to your worship services. Throughout this book we have suggested that such a gradual approach may be the best strategy in most congregations.

To move gradually to eliminate sexism in worship may mean that at first you simply take out all obviously sexist references in your worship: You will stop using hymns and prayers that refer to man and mankind, brothers, sons, and so on. This need not be especially difficult since there are many excellent prayers and hymns that are already non-sexist as we have noted earlier. (See also p. 108.) When talking of God you will simply use the word *God* or a non-sexist synonym such as *creator* rather than a sexist word like *father* or even the pronoun *he*. The same careful use of words will be followed in the sermon.

Only after some real communication has had a chance to happen, in small groups and on a one-to-one basis, will you want to move on to occasionally bringing both the masculine and the feminine attributes into the service with references to

God as mother/father, or she/he.

You will want also to take this opportunity of changing your worship to liberate it in ways other than simply the use of language. We have talked of liberating the leadership of the liturgy and how essential this is; it is important to pick the persons who will be leading in a new way with great care. They should be persons who are highly respected in your faith community. You should be willing to spend time with them (or have another knowledgeable person spend time with them) so that they do an outstanding job of leading worship—better than what has been done.

You may also want to introduce other changes that will help free your services and make them more meaningful for the congregation as a whole. New music, the use of film and dance, discussion sermons, and so forth, may be things you'll want to try. Be careful, however, that you don't overwhelm your congregation with change. You may end up having your people identifying non-sexist worship with a particular type of music or sermon, and that would be most unfortunate.

On the other hand, sometimes introducing several changes at once can help with the acceptance of each of the changes. For example, if you know that your congregation is wanting a different kind of music you might introduce that at the same time you begin non-sexist services. The congregation would then be much more likely to be affirmative to the non-sexist change too.

The principle we just illustrated can be stated in a simple rule: *Where possible, mix a popular and unpopular change together to achieve maximum acceptance of the unpopular change.*

For example, if you want to introduce new songbooks into your congregation, you can best do this your first Sunday by singing a song from the books that you know your people like very much. They will then feel much better toward the new books which they might have rejected completely had you in troduced them with a totally unfamiliar song.

As you work with the people in your congregation, do not let some of them persuade you that doing nothing is moving gradually ahead. It may be extremely important to move slowly in bringing about liturgical change, but you should always be able to point to some progress, some work that is being done. Often the opponents of change attempt to neutralize the changers by convincing them they are progressing when nothing is being done. That is false and should be rejected firmly by you.

No matter how carefully you engineer your program of change, you will probably run into some persons who are against it. It is important to listen to these persons and try to discover why they are opposed to the changes. With careful listening you may learn about some of the problems in your own techniques in working for change. This can help you as you continue your work. You may also discover that the persons who are objecting do so for reasons that are often quite nonrational. The individuals may cover their objections with seemingly rational reasons or by appealing to numbers ("So many people are upset in our church now"). But when these arguments are shown to be ineffective, these persons may still continue to object, always trying to find a new rationalization. Often such objection springs from a deep nostalgia, a worship of the past when everything was stable and everyone seemed happy. Such persons often say, "The worship service was the one stable rock I had to cling to, and now you want to take that away too."

Try to help these persons know that you understand some of their deep feelings and fears. Perhaps you may restate their ideas to make sure you understand what they are saying and feeling and so that they will know that you understand. Then try to help them realize that liberating the liturgy won't destroy their faith but will actually help to make it more solid. It will also be a powerful way of helping others who are now turned off by worship languages and practices to discover a strong and viable faith. Such appeals to the new strength that the objecting person can find in a changed liturgy and to the sacrifice that these persons can make to help others can be powerfully convincing.

No matter what you do or say, however, you must be prepared to accept the fact that perhaps some people will be so turned off by change in the liturgy that they will leave your church and go elsewhere. This is not necessarily a bad thing. It is dishonest for a person to remain a part of a worshipping community if that community is worshipping in a way that that person feels is wrong or at least not meaningful. An increasing number of women and men are realizing this, and if changes away from a sexist liturgy are not made soon, they will be the ones who will leave. Often a person who is extremely dissatisfied with a church's worship will show dissatisfaction with most of the other activities of the church and actually act as a divisive force within the community. Both for the good of the community and for that particular person, a change to another congregation more in keeping with that person's beliefs and practices is in order.

You must also be prepared to accept the fact that if you have really been successful in eliminating sexism in your worship and liberating your liturgy you will suddenly discover that many women in your church are experiencing worship and the Christian faith on a new and deeper level than ever before. A new excitement should begin to sweep through your church as both men and women begin to discover the freeing power that is present when the old stereotypes of sex roles and God-concept are broken. You will also discover that new persons are coming to your church—attracted by its honesty, by its willingness to face one of the crucial issues of our day and do something concrete and positive about it. You'll begin to experience what the apostle Paul dreamed about when he said that there is neither Jew nor Gentile, slave nor free, male nor female, but all are one in Christ Jesus.

Appendix A

A LISTING OF NON-SEXIST HYMNS

Our criteria for choosing the hymns below was their non-sexist language. We made no attempt to screen hymns on any other basis, be it theology or musical style. We did choose only hymns that appeared in at least two of the hymnals. Therefore, in all of the hymnals, there are other non-sexist hymns that appear. We provide this list for you only as a starter. You should check your own hymnal and make your own list. We determined that a hymn had non-sexist language on the following basis:

1. No masculine words used generically such as "mankind," "brotherhood," "sons of God," and so forth.

2. No masculine references to God such as "Lord" or "Father" and no references to God's reign as a "kingdom."

3. No masculine references to Christ other than "he," "him," or "his."

4. No references to the Church or to objects as "she."

In preparing these charts we used several of the major Protestant denominations' most popular hymnals as well as the Roman Catholic *Hymnal for Young Christians*. We did not attempt to be inclusive, but merely representative, in choosing hymnals. If your denomination is not represented, you can make your own column for your hymnal. And whether or not your hymnal is listed, we encourage you as soon as you can to do your own chart.

	Baptist Hymnal Southern Baptist American Baptist	*Christian Worship* Disciples of Christ American Baptist	*The Book of Hymns* United Methodist	*Pilgrim Hymnal* United Church of Christ	*Service Book and Hymnal* The Lutheran Churches	*The Hymnal* United Presbyterian
Art Thou Weary	*	*	*		*	*
Author of Life Divine			*		*	*
Be Known to Us In Breaking Bread	*		*	*		*
Beneath the Cross of Jesus	*	*	*	*	*	*
Bread of the World in Mercy Broken	*	*	*	*	*	*
Breathe on Me, Breath of God	*		*	*	*	*
Christ, Whose Glory Fills the Skies	*		*	*	*	*
Come Down, O Love Divine			*	*	*	
Come Let Us Tune Our Loftiest Song	*		*			
Come, Ye Disconsolate	*	*	*		*	*
Fling Out the Banner	*	*		*	*	*
Go, Tell It on the Mountain			*	*		
God, That Madest Earth and Heaven	*	*	*	*	*1	*

¹Has variant reading of third verse which is sexist.

	Baptist Hymnal Southern Baptist American Baptist	Christian Worship Disciples of Christ American Baptist	The Book of Hymns United Methodist	Pilgrim Hymnal United Church of Christ	Service Book and Hymnal The Lutheran Churches	The Hymnal United Presbyterian
Guide Me, O Thou Great Jehovah	*	*	*	*	*	*
I Heard the Voice of Jesus Say	*	*	*		*	*
I Know That My Redeemer Lives		*	*		*	
I Look to Thee in Every Need			*	*	*	*
I Love to Tell the Story	*	*	*	*	*	*
In Heavenly Love Abiding	*	*	*	*	*	*
In the Cross of Christ I Glory	*	*	*	*	*	*
In the Hour of Trial	*	*	*	*	*	*
Jesus Calls Us O'er the Tumult	*	*	*	*	*	*
Jesus, Lover of My Soul	*	*	*	*	*	*
Jesus, Savior, Pilot Me	*	*	*	*	*	*
Jesus, Thy Boundless Love to Me	*	*	*		*	*
Just As I Am	*	*	*	*	*	*

	Baptist Hymnal / Southern Baptist / American Baptist	Christian Worship / Disciples of Christ / American Baptist	The Book of Hymns / United Methodist	Pilgrim Hymnal / United Church of Christ	Service Book and Hymnal / The Lutheran Churches	The Hymnal / United Presbyterian
Lead, Kindly Light	*	*	*	*	*	*
Love Divine, All Loves Excelling	*	*	*	*	*	*
More Love to Thee, O Christ	*	*	*	*	*	*
Must Jesus Bear the Cross Alone	*	*	*			
My Faith Looks Up to Thee	*	*	*	*	*	*
My Hope Is Built on Nothing Less	*		*		*	
Nearer, My God, to Thee	*	*	*	*	*	*
Now the Day Is Over	*	*	*	*	*	*
O Grant Us Light that We May Know		*				*
O Love That Wilt Not Let Me Go	*	*	*	*	*	*
O Perfect Love, All Human Thought Transcending	*		*	*	*	*
O Sometimes the Shadows are Deep	*		*			
Open My Eyes, That I May See	*		*			

	Baptist Hymnal Southern Baptist American Baptist	*Christian Worship* Disciples of Christ American Baptist	*The Book of Hymns* United Methodist	*Pilgrim Hymnal* United Church of Christ	*Service Book and Hymnal* The Lutheran Churches	*The Hymnal* United Presbyterian
Our God to Whom We Turn				*	*	
Pass Me Not, O Gentle Savior			*		*	
Peace, Perfect Peace			*		*	*
Purer in Heart, O God	*	*				
Rock of Ages, Cleft for Me	*	*	*	*	*	*
Sing Them Over Again to Me	*	*	*			
Spirit Divine, Attend Our Prayers	*	*	*	*		*
Still, Still With Thee	*	*	*	*	*	*
There Is a Fountain Filled With Blood	*		*		*	*
This Is the Day of Light		*				*
Thou, Whose Unmeasured Temple stands			*		*	*
We Are Climbing Jacob's Ladder			*	*1		

The following hymns are from *Hymnal for Young Christians* published by F.E.L. Church Publications, Ltd.

Appendix B

SUGGESTED READING: HELPFUL RESOURCES

Books

Daly, Mary. *The Church and the Second Sex.* New York: Harper & Row, 1968.

Doely, Sarah Bentley. *Women's Liberation and the Church.* New York: Association Press, 1970.

Faxon, Alicia Craig. *Women and Jesus.* Philadelphia: United Church Press, 1973.

McGrath, O.D., Sister Alberta Magnus. *What a Modern Catholic Believes About Women.* Chicago: Thomas More Associates, 1972.

Swidler, Arlene. *Woman in a Man's Church.* New York: Paulist Press, 1972.

Articles

Christ, Carol, and Marilyn Collins. "Shattering the Idols of Men: Theology from the Perspective of Women's Experience." *Reflection,* a Journal of Opinion at Yale Divinity School and Berkley Divinity School, May, 1972.

Collins, Sheila D. "Toward a Feminist Theology." *The Christian Century,* August 2, 1972, pp. 796–799.

Goldstein, Valerie. "The Human Situation: A Feminine View." *Journal of Religion,* April, 1960, pp. 100–112.

Hardesty, Nancy. "Women: Second Class Citizens?" *Eternity,* January, 1971.

Hoppin, Ruth. "Games Bible Translators Play." *Women and Religion*, a packet of educational materials by The National Organization for Women, Ecumenical Task Force on Women and Religion, 1957 East 73rd Street, Chicago, Illinois.

Mollenkott, Virginia R. "Woman's Liberation and the Bible." *The Christian Herald*, December, 1972.

Scroggs, Robin. "Paul: Chauvinist or Liberationist?" *The Christian Century*, March 15, 1972, pp. 307–309.

Swidler, Leonard. "Jesus Was a Feminist." *Catholic World*, January, 1971, pp. 177–183.

Magazines

The Christian Ministry, May 1971. Special issue on women and the church.

Concern, May–June, 1971. Published by the United Presbyterian Women and the YWCA. Special issue on women's liberation in a biblical perspective.